The
Poems
of Hesiod

The
Poems
of Hesiod

Translated with
Introduction and Comments by
R.M. Frazer

ILLUSTRATED BY MARY SUE RONIGER

UNIVERSITY OF OKLAHOMA PRESS: NORMAN

BY R. M. FRAZER

(Translated with Introduction and Notes) *The Trojan War: The Chronicles of Dictys of Crete and Dares the Phrygian* (Bloomington and London, 1966)

This book has been published with the aid of a grant from the Andrew W. Mellon Foundation.

Library of Congress Cataloging in Publication Data

Hesiod.
  The poems of Hesiod.

  Bibliography: p. 143
  Includes index.
  Contents: Theogony—Works and days.
  I. Hesiod. Works and days. English. 1983. II. Frazer, R. M. (Richard McIlwaine), 1931–   . III. Title.
PA4010.E5T5 1983   881′.01   82-40451
ISBN: 0-8061-1846-6

Copyright © 1983 by the University of Oklahoma Press, Norman, Publishing Division of the University. All rights reserved. Manufactured in the U.S.A.

13   14   15   16   17   18   19   20

Contents

INTRODUCTION

Hesiod's Life, Poetry, and Times	3
Some Near Eastern Influences and Parallels	8
The Succession Myth	8
Wisdom Literature	10
Prophecy	11
Hesiod's Religious Thought	12
Some Features of Hesiod's Style	15
The Present Translation and Commentary	17

Theogony

An Introductory Hymn to the Muses (lines 1–115)	23
The Earliest Powers: Chaos, Gaia, Eros, and Night (lines 116–25)	30
The Children of Gaia	32
Ouranos, Pontos, and the Titans (lines 126–38)	32
The Kyklopes and the Hundred-Handers (lines 139–53)	33
Kronos Castrates Ouranos: The Rise of the Titans and the Birth of Aphrodite (lines 154–210)	34
The Progeny of Night (lines 211–32)	38
The Descendants of Pontos	40
His Children: Nereus, Thaumas, Phorkys, Keto, and Eurybia (lines 233–39)	40

The Daughters of Nereus (lines 240-64)   41
The Children of Thaumas (lines 265-69)   42
The Progeny of Phorkys and Keto: The Monsters
    (lines 270-336)   43
Beneficent Titanic Powers   48
    The Children of Okeanos and Tethys (lines 337-70)   48
    The Children of Hyperion and Theia (lines 371-74)   50
    The Descendants of Krios and Eurybia. Styx and
        Her Children (lines 375-403)   51
    The Descendants of Koios and Phoibe. The Great
        Goddess Hekate (lines 404-52)   53
The Rise of Zeus   56
    The Birth of Zeus and the Other Olympians, the
        Children of Kronos and Rhea (lines 453-500)   56
    Zeus Obtains the Kyklopes' Thunderbolts (lines
        501-506)   60
Zeus Outwits Prometheus   61
    The Maleficent Sons of Iapetos (lines 507-34)   61
    The Creation of Woman (lines 535-616)   64
The War with the Titans   68
    Zeus Obtains the Hundred-Handers' Assistance
        (lines 617-73)   68
    The Final Battle (lines 674-721)   71
The Description of the Underworld (lines 722-819)   74
Zeus Defeats His Last Enemy, the Monster Typhoeus
    (lines 820-80)   78
The Kingship of Zeus and His Marriages (lines
    881-929)   83
More Unions of Zeus and Other Gods and Goddesses
    (lines 930-1022)   86

Works and Days

An Introductory Hymn to Zeus (lines 1-10)   93
The Two Kinds of Eris (lines 11-41)   94
The Prometheus-Pandora Story (lines 42-105)   97
The Story of the Ages of Man (lines 106-202)   101

The Fable of the Hawk and the Nightingale (lines
   202–12)   105
An Exhortation to Justice (lines 213–85)   106
An Exhortation to Work (lines 286–319)   111
Advice on Being Successful (lines 320–80)   113
The Farmer's Calendar   116
  Introduction (lines 381–413)   116
  Autumn (lines 414–92)   118
  Winter (lines 493–563)   122
  Spring and Summer (lines 564–617)   126
A Guide for the Merchant Sailor. Hesiod's Witness
  (lines 618–94)   130
Social and Religious Advice (lines 695–764)   135
The *Days* (lines 765–828)   139

SELECT BIBLIOGRAPHY   143

INDEX   147

Illustrations

Eros	31
Atlas and Prometheus	62
Zeus Fighting Typhoeus	79
The Bad Eris (Strife)	95
Justice (Dike) Defeating Injustice (Adikia)	107
Two Men Fighting over a Tripod-Cauldron	132

Preface

"Besides Homer, there is Hesiod." These words of Zimmern, quoted by M. L. West at the beginning of his fine commentary on the *Theogony*, contain much truth. Hesiod is a very important poet. It is for this reason that his poems, the *Theogony* and the *Works and Days*, deserve to be presented as accurately and attractively as possible. I have tried to do this by giving a translation that is faithful to the matter and spirit of the original, and by offering sufficient comment on the text to make it understandable and enjoyable to the average reader. The poems have been divided into sections for easy study, and after each section a Comment appears. An Introduction provides necessary background information on Hesiod and his poetry. The discussion in the Introduction and the Comments might have been fuller, more detailed, more expansive on controversial issues, but I have feared that by saying more I might only cloud the reader's enjoyment of the poems themselves.

I am especially grateful to Carroll E. Mace for his encouragement and valuable criticism. An expert on the Quiché dance dramas of Rabinal, in Guatemala, he gave the same careful attention to my very different subject as he does to his own. My thanks are also due to Joe Park Poe, Thomas A. Montgomery, and the readers of the University of Oklahoma Press for suggesting improvements; and to Jessie Poesch for advising me on the illustrations and recommending an artist. Finally, I am indebted to this artist, Mary Sue Roniger, for her excellent pen-and-ink drawings.

Proper names are usually given in direct transliteration. Thus "Aineias" appears instead of "Aeneas," "Krete" instead of "Crete," "Kypros" instead of "Cyprus," "Oidipous" instead of "Oedipus," and "Iason" instead of "Jason." Similarly, "aigis" —a word used to describe Zeus—is given instead of "aegis." The following words, however, appear in their common English forms: Apollo, Delphi, Mycenaean, and Phoenician.

Introduction

Hesiod is an early Greek poet who probably flourished around 700 B.C. Two poems by him survive complete, the *Theogony* and the *Works and Days* (hereafter referred to as *Theog.* and *W.D.*). The *Shield of Herakles*, which was attributed to him in antiquity, must be dated long after he lived, since it shows the influence of works of art of the sixth century B.C. Eleven other poems of which we possess only fragments, and two for which we have only the titles, were attributed to him, but it is impossible to say which, if any, is genuine. The most important of these is the *Catalog of Women*, which was appended to *Theog.* Another, the *Divination by Birds*, was appended to *W.D.* None of these other poems was ever so popular or influential as *Theog.* or *W.D.*

Some scholars doubt whether the same person composed *Theog.* and *W.D.*, but strong evidence in favor of common authorship is provided by references, one in each poem, to the poet's initial inspiration by the Muses. The poet of *Theog.*, in lines 22–23, introducing himself by the name of Hesiod, tells us that he was first inspired by the Muses in the foothills of Mount Helikon; and the poet of *W.D.*, in lines 646–59, tells us that he dedicated a tripod-cauldron to the Muses on the spot of Mount Helikon where they had first inspired him. Accordingly, it seems very likely that the same person, Hesiod, composed *W.D.* as well as *Theog.* This conclusion is strengthened

3

by a close study of the poems, which reveal the same unique personality—that of a deeply religious man concerned with the problems of justice and fate.

The differences between the poems can be explained by their different subject matter. *Theog.* deals with the high epic theme of the creation of the divine order of the world under the direction of Zeus, while *W.D.* is a didactic poem on justice and work with reference to Hesiod's own life. This difference in subject matter produces a difference in style, *Theog.* being more influenced by epic conventions and seeming more stilted or wooden, while *W.D.* seems the more modern, freewheeling poem.

W.D. is probably the later of the two poems, for it contains passages that apparently assume a knowledge of *Theog.* For instance, *W.D.* 11ff., where we are told that there is a good Eris (Strife) as well as a bad one, seems to be an elaboration on *Theog.* 225ff., where only the bad Eris is mentioned; and the version of Prometheus's tricking of Zeus in *W.D.* 47ff. seems to be an abridgment of this story as more fully told in *Theog.* 565ff. Moreover, we naturally expect a poet to describe his initial inspiration in his earliest poem in order to show his credentials, and this Hesiod does in *Theog.* 22ff.

Hesiod is the first Greek and, therefore, the first European we can know as a real person, for, unlike Homer, he tells us about himself in his poems. The most important autobiographical passage is *W.D.* 631–59, to which we have already referred. Here we learn that Hesiod's father had once sailed across the Aigean Sea from Kyme (on the coast of Asia Minor, in Aiolis) to Greece and settled in Askra, near Mount Helikon, in Boiotia; that the farthest Hesiod himself had ever sailed was across the narrow stretch of water from Aulis, in Boiotia, to Chalkis, on the island of Euboia, when he participated in the funeral games of Amphidamas; and that at these games he won as the first prize in the poetry contest the tripod-cauldron that he dedicated to the Muses on Mount Helikon. We can infer from his having sailed no farther than from Aulis to Chalkis that he was born in Askra and not in Kyme.

Another important autobiographical passage is *W.D.* 37–

39, where we are told about a dispute with his brother, Perses, over their inheritance. The fact of this inheritance shows that their father must have met with some success as a farmer in Askra. Their case was brought before the nobles who presided as judges in their area, probably sitting at Thespiai, the main town of southern Boiotia. (In the archaic period the nobles formed the class from which judges normally came; Hesiod called them *basilēes*, "kings," which I use in the text, a term inherited from the Bronze Age when kings had much greater power.) Perses came off with more than his fair share by bribing these judges, and then seems to have threatened Hesiod with another suit over the same matter. This is the background, the occasion, that spurred Hesiod to compose *W.D.*

The occasion for which *Theog.* was composed is more difficult to determine. An attractive suggestion, for which West argues,[1] is that it was the poetry contest at the funeral games of Amphidamas. Perhaps *Theog.* 89–103, where the Muses are described as bringers of forgetfulness to those grieving the loss of a loved one, was composed with this funeral in mind.

There is little else we can learn about Hesiod from his poems except that he was a successful farmer and a rather gloomy though not humorless man. In *W.D.* 299 he implies that Perses lays claim to noble descent, but this may be only a piece of sarcasm. One suspects from his concern for the bachelor's lot (*Theog.* 603ff.) and some rather unflattering remarks on women (cf. *W.D.* 373ff.) that he was never married. When he speaks as if he had a son (*W.D.* 270–72) we should not necessarily infer that he really had one.

In order to get a fuller picture of him we must try to understand him in relation to his times, and this brings us to the problem of when he lived. We are probably safe in dating him between 750 and 650 B.C. It seems likely that he lived after the Greeks adopted the alphabet during the first half of the eighth century B.C., that is, after around 750 B.C., for it is hard to imagine that his poems were not written down soon after composition, since otherwise their autobiographical passages would probably have been omitted or altered in oral transmission. For a date before which he must have lived we have the evidence of seventh-century lyric poetry that clearly shows his influence, and this puts him before around 650 B.C. There is an ancient tradition, which I would like to accept, that he was a contemporary of Homer, who is put in the latter half of the eighth century. Arguments that he influenced Homer or that Homer influenced him are not convincing, since both of them may have drawn on the same epic tradition.

Our best evidence for dating him more precisely is connected with the passage on the funeral games of Amphidamas. An ancient commentator notes that this Amphidamas was killed in a sea battle during the Lelantine War fought between Chalkis and Eretria. The exact date of this war is still in dispute, but it seems likely that it ended in the last decade of the eighth century.[2] If this is so, the poem (perhaps *Theog.*) with which Hesiod won his victory in the poetry contest must belong to the late eighth century; and the later poem, *W.D.*, must be dated later in the eighth century, or perhaps in the early seventh century. A date for the poetry contest in the last decade of the eighth century is consistent with the fact that tripod-cauldrons of the type won by Hesiod were still in fashion during this time.[3] We can thus put the most important part of his life—his formative years until he became well known as a poet—in the last part of the eighth century.

The eighth century is the time of the great Greek awakening after the period of relative darkness ushered in by the fall of the old Mycenaean kingdoms around 1125 B.C. The political unit was now the city-state and not, as in the Mycenaean age, the large feudal kingdom; rulers holding sway over a wide area had passed away and yielded their power to aristocratic alliances of minor kings or lords. This was, however, an age of expanding horizons, when the Greeks were colonizing the western Mediterranean, learning to write, and building their first temples.

The Greek renaissance was beginning, but we must beware of reading back into this time what we know of the later classical period. The temples were usually small and crudely made, often of mud brick; the invention of the Doric and Ionic orders lay in the future. By the end of the eighth century pottery was beginning to move out of its geometric into its orientalizing phase, but the black- and red-figure styles were yet to be seen. Representations of the human body lacked the realism of later classical art; the first stage of Greek sculpture (the Daidalic style) does not begin until the second quarter of the seventh century. We know from Homer and Hesiod of beautiful dances and songs and above all of the brilliance of epic poetry, but the development of tragedy and comedy belongs to a later time. The standard of exchange was cattle, valued utensils, and bars of metal; the invention of coinage comes later. There was no philosophy and no science of history or geography. Yet, all this being said, we should emphasize again that Hesiod lived at the beginning of the Greek renaissance.

In later times, probably owing to Athenian prejudice, Boiotia had a reputation for backwardness. The Boiotians, however, could pride themselves on having produced some of the most famous heroes of Greek mythology, such as Oidipous of Thebes, and they seem to have developed catalog poetry as their special contribution to the Greek epic. The Athenian taunt of "Boiotian pig" no doubt referred to the slowness of the Boiotians, but it might also be used to describe their fatness, that is, wealth. Their slowness might be thought of, more sympathetically, as conservatism, which is perhaps another reason, in addition to their sufficiency of land, why they sent out no colonies. They preferred to stay at home and go their own sweet ways, while being easily able to keep abreast of new ideas and inventions, such as the alphabet, through more adventuresome neighbors.

Boiotia was good country.[4] When Hesiod complains about the badness of Askra (*W.D.* 639f.), we should take what he says with a grain of salt, for he is by nature a grumbler. He is usually described as a peasant, but the terms semiaristocrat or middling farmer are probably more accurate.[5] No landlord was over him. The land he farmed was his, and he was the owner of oxen and slaves. We can imagine him as a proudly

independent farmer, whose success at farming made him an
independent poet unbeholden to any noble patron and free to
speak his mind.

SOME NEAR EASTERN INFLUENCES AND PARALLELS

The Succession Myth

Near Eastern influence on Hesiod is most convincingly seen in
what is called the Succession Myth of *Theog.*, for close parallels
are found in Babylonian, Hittite, and Phoenician literature.[6]
This is rather complicated material, but it will be worth our
while to review the most important points of comparison. The
Babylonian epic of creation is *Enuma Elish (When on High)*,
whose composition is now put after 1100 B.C., though much
of it was probably known much earlier. According to this epic,
Apsu and Tiamat give rise to five generations of descendants,
the last three of which are ruled over respectively by the sky
god Anu, by Ea, and by Marduk. These three gods are similar
to the three ruling gods in the Succession Myth of *Theog.*, Anu
being comparable to Ouranos, Ea to Kronos, and Marduk to
Zeus. Marduk comes to power by defeating Tiamat, a sea
monster, in single combat. This event is comparable to the
single combat between Zeus and his last enemy, the monster
Typhoeus.

The Hittites flourished in Asia Minor in the fourteenth
and thirteenth centuries B.C. They were the conquerors of
the Hurrians, whose civilization influenced them greatly, as
is shown by their mythological texts which are for the most
part translations of earlier Hurrian myths. Of special interest
to us are the Kingship in Heaven text and the *Song of Ulli-
kummi*. The Kingship in Heaven text tells of four generations
ruled over respectively by Alalu, by the sky god Anu, by
Kumarbi, and by the storm god. It is clear that Anu is com-
parable to Ouranos, Kumarbi to Kronos, and the storm god
to Zeus. Moreover, Kumarbi overcomes Anu by biting off
and swallowing his genitals—an event comparable to Kronos's

castration of Ouranos and his swallowing of his own children. The *Song of Ullikummi* tells how a stone monster, Ullikummi, whom Kumarbi begets, is defeated by the storm god. Again, we can compare Zeus's defeat of the monster Typhoeus. These two myths, taken together, show more similarities to *Theog.* than *Enuma Elish* does, for they share with it not only the succession of rulers and the story of the monster who threatens the rule of the final king but also the castration and swallowing motifs.

The Phoenicians are the same people as the Canaanites, who inhabited Palestine before the invasion of the Israelites. Although we know of their mythology from later Greek reports, our most important sources are texts found at Ugarit (modern Ras Shamra), which can be dated to the fourteenth century B.C. The striking similarity between Phoenician and Hittite mythology is probably owing to the influence of the Hurrians on both of these peoples. Again there are four generations of gods: first a highest god, then the sky god (comparable to Ouranos), then El (comparable to Kronos), and finally the storm god Baal (comparable to Zeus). El castrates the sky god, and Baal, using two clubs made by a divine craftsman (we are reminded of the Kyklopes who make the thunderbolts of Zeus), defeats Yamm (Sea, a monster of chaos comparable to Typhoeus). In another, apparently parallel version, Baal destroys the seven-headed monster Lotan. We can compare (see the Comment on *Theog.* 820–80) the destruction by God of the many-headed sea monster Leviathan in the Bible, a book that sometimes shows the influence of Phoenician mythology in poetic passages.[7]

The origin of the Succession Myth in the Near East is shown by its very early and widespread popularity there. When and how it came to Greece is hard to say. Perhaps it came during the Mycenaean period through Ugarit; perhaps later through Asia Minor or Kypros (Cyprus), or a place on the Phoenician coast now called Al Mina. Greek pottery is found at Al Mina beginning around 825 B.C., much of it after 750 B.C. being from Euboia.

Wisdom Literature

There are two main Near Eastern traditions of wisdom litera-
ture, the Mesopotamian and the Egyptian, both of which can
be traced back into the third millennium B.C.[8] From Meso-
potamia we have Sumerian books of instruction, collections of
proverbs, and such works as the Babylonian *Counsels of Wisdom*
(1500–1200 B.C.); from Egypt such works as the *Instruction
of Ptah-hotep* (around 2450 B.C.) and the *Instruction of Amen-
em-Opet* (before 1100 B.C.). The best-known example of Near
Eastern wisdom literature is the biblical book of Proverbs,
much of which may well date to the period of the monarchy
(1000–600 B.C.) and in particular to the reign of the wise king
Solomon to whom it is attributed.

Wise men were highly educated, literate poets and teachers
who often served as the advisers of kings. Their teachings,
based as they were on reason, had a universal appeal and easily
crossed national boundaries. The typical book of instruction is
addressed by a father to his son. It contrasts the wise man and
the fool, of whom there are many kinds, and teaches by pre-
cepts and proverbs. We are given advice on such topics as
friendship and marriage, and are told to avoid legal disputes,
to make our living by honest hard work, to show kindness to
the poor, and to control our tongue. The major premise of the
wise man is that eventually good deeds are rewarded and bad
deeds punished. In Egyptian literature this idea of retributive
justice is expressed by the word *Maat*, which is variously trans-
lated "Justice," "Truth," or "Order."

Similarities of form and content make it likely that Near
Eastern wisdom literature has influenced *W.D.* Perses is pic-
tured as a manifold fool, and the wise man Hesiod exhorts
him to stop doing wrong and get down to work, gives him
advice on friendship and marriage, and tells him that he should
be kind to the poor and hold his tongue. In one respect, how-
ever, *W.D.* is different from Near Eastern books of instruction:
it contains sections on the technical subjects of farming, sailing,
and significant days, which in the Near East are treated in
separate works.

The teachings of *W.D.* are enlivened by proverbs for which there are often parallels in the wisdom literature of the Near East. For instance, we can compare *W.D.* 265f.:

> He who devises harm for another is harming himself,
> and from the plan that is harmful most harm comes
>   to the planner.

with Proverbs 26:27:

> If a man digs a pit, he will fall into it;
> if he rolls a stone, it will roll back upon him.

Both of these sayings are concerned with retributive justice. The equivalent for Hesiod of the Egyptian *Maat* is the orderly government of the world under the direction of Zeus.

The fable is another form of Near Eastern wisdom literature, and there are Near Eastern parallels to the fable of the hawk and the nightingale told in *W.D.* 202-12. The hawk, while carrying off the nightingale, rebukes her for shrieking. We can compare a Sumerian fable about a butcher who, while slaughtering a pig, rebukes it for squealing.[9] Somewhat similar is the biblical fable in 2 Kings 14:9, in which a wild beast is said to have trampled down a thistle of Lebanon that had had the presumption to try to marry its son to a daughter of a cedar of Lebanon.

We should note that cleverness or trickery can be considered a sort of wisdom. Although it is of a lower order than the wisdom of ethical or technical knowledge, it is useful in proving one's superiority, especially against enemies. It is the wisdom of the fable and folktale, and frequently appears in epic stories of conflict. For instance, in Hesiod's story of the creation of woman (Pandora), Prometheus tries, though in vain, to trick Zeus. We can compare the role of the serpent, the cleverest of all the wild creatures, in the similar story of the fall of man in Genesis 3.

Prophecy

It is easy to see why Hesiod is sometimes compared with the classical Hebrew prophets beginning with Amos in the eighth century B.C. These prophets were called by God to rebuke their people for doing injustice. Moreover, they were brilliant poets, who were often influenced by wisdom literature; and they spoke out fearlessly against their kings.

Hesiod's conviction that Zeus rewards justice and punishes injustice enables him to speak prophetically. For instance, he foresees that the men of the iron race will meet with a catastrophic end because of their disregard of all moral values (*W.D.* 180-201); and that the nobles (called "kings" in the text) who rule with straight decisions of justice will cause their cities to prosper, while those who rule with crooked decisions of injustice will cause their cities to perish (*W.D.* 225-47). His saying that "he who swears truly creates for his family future prosperity" (*W.D.* 285) is later found in a prophecy of the Delphic oracle reported by Herodotos (6.86).

Hesiod can call the nobles to account because he, no less than they, can claim to be inspired by the Muses to speak what is true and just (cf. *Theog.* 80-96). When he addresses them as fools, he no doubt does so not only as a wisdom teacher but also as a prophetic poet. We can compare the Delphic oracle reported by Herodotos (1.85) in which King Kroisos is addressed as "Kroisos, you great fool." Hesiod, perhaps being more cautious than Delphi, reserves the use of "great fool" for Perses.

HESIOD'S RELIGIOUS THOUGHT

How each of the gods came into being, whether they always existed, and what are their forms, the Greeks did not know until yesterday or the day before, so to speak; for Hesiod and Homer, I believe, lived four hundred years before my time and no more, and they are the ones who made a theogony for the Greeks and gave the gods their epithets and apportioned to them their honors and functions and showed how they look.

This statement by Herodotos (2.53) probably dates Hesiod and Homer a hundred years too early, and no doubt attributes to them what in many respects is the culmination of a long epic tradition, but otherwise it deserves to be taken very seriously. We must be careful, however, to understand it correctly. It does not say that Hesiod and Homer invented the gods and Greek religion, but only that they gave the Greeks a clear picture of the forms, functions, and relationships of the gods.

The world of early Greek religion is full of gods. Everywhere—in the physical world, in human relationships, and in the individual's heart and mind—powers are at work that are wonderful and therefore divine. Not even an inspired poet is able to know and name them all, as Hesiod admits in the case of the river gods (*Theog.* 369f.) and as he implies in his belated recognition of the good Eris (*W.D.* 11ff.). But not all the gods are equally powerful; there is a hierarchy, at the top of which are the Olympians ruled over by Zeus.

A great gulf separates gods and men. The gods are immortal and live blessed lives, while death is the fate of men, who are given either a lot of nothing but ills or at best a mixed lot of goods and ills. This idea of man's fate is vividly described in *Iliad* 24.525ff., where Achilleus (Achilles) tells Priam about the jars of Zeus. Zeus has two jars in his storeroom, one of ills and the other of goods. To some men he gives a mixture from both jars, but to others he gives only from the jar of ills. To no one does he give only from the jar of goods; in other words, no one is granted a life like that of the gods. The same idea appears in *Theog.* 600ff., where every man's dilemma is described in terms of the bachelor's choices with regard to marriage. The man who either remains a bachelor or marries well can expect a mixed lot, but he who marries badly will get an all-bad lot; there is no such thing as an all-good lot.

One of the words for "lot" in Greek is *moira*, and the Moirai are the Fates. It seems to have made little difference to an ancient Greek whether he spoke of Zeus or the Moirai or the gods in general as being responsible for men's fates. But the thoughtful believer must have felt the problem of whether Zeus, the greatest of the gods, was subject to fate. Hesiod seems to be trying to solve this problem in *Theog.* when he first describes the Moirai as the daughters of Night (219) and then as the daughters of Themis and Zeus (904ff.).

Sane men, according to ancient Greek belief, remember the gulf that separates them from the gods and beware of acting with hybris. The man of hybris, feeling superior and lacking a proper sense of shame, transgresses against the rights of others. His wrongdoing begins in self-delusion and is very similar to the biblical sin of pride that goes before destruction. Hybris inevitably results in nemesis, which is the avenging disapproval of the gods and one's fellow human beings. Again we see that the belief in retribution is fundamental. In the long run the power of Justice, a very important divinity for Hesiod, always triumphs over Hybris (cf. *W.D.* 213ff.).[10]

In considering Hesiod's religious seriousness we must face the problem of how literally he intends us to take his account of the gods in *Theog.* It seems likely that his main concern was to describe the significance of the various gods, and that he was sometimes doubtful about what name or relationship might best serve this purpose. Thus he may not have felt that all the names he gives the Muses are the only possible ones to express their natures as beautiful dancers and singers; and the fact that he gives the Moirai two different parentages should warn us against assuming that every relationship he describes is the only possible one that he could imagine. We should remember that for the ancient Greeks the proper worship of the gods was always more important than any mythology about them.

Hesiod is sometimes seen as a forerunner of the earliest Greek philosophers, for an interest in cosmogony is a part of his religious thought.[11] These philosophers believed that the world as we know it evolved from an original self-moving source, and that the regular interaction of its various elements is to be explained in terms of natural law. It is arguable that Chaos is the original source of everything for Hesiod; and the natural law of the philosophers reminds us of his belief that the world is governed by Zeus in accordance with justice.

SOME FEATURES OF HESIOD'S STYLE

The first thing to be said about Hesiod's style is that it is essentially the same as Homer's. This is owing to the fact that both of them, regardless of whether or not they could write, composed in the formula tradition of oral epic poetry. They thus used the same artificial language, the same meter, and many of the same epic formulas.

The language is an amalgam of many different forms, an invention of the epic poets.[12] It is based largely on the Ionic dialect, but also draws on other dialects, such as the Aiolic. Some of its forms are found only in epic poetry. Since Hesiod spoke Boiotian, which is a non-Ionic, half-Aiolic dialect, this language must have sounded somewhat stranger to him than to a native Ionian like Homer.

The meter of Greek epic poetry (and also Latin) is the dactylic hexameter. In this meter dactyls (a long and two short syllables) prevail over spondees (two longs) in the first five feet, and the final sixth foot is always a spondee. My translation of *Theog.* 25 is a good approximation to this meter: "Muses who sing on Olympos, the daughters of Zeus of the Aigis."

Oral epic poetry is characterized by its use of such formulas as "the daughters of Zeus of the Aigis." This expression appears at three other places in Hesiod and at four places in Homer. When an oral poet wanted to say something in a given part of the hexameter line, he often used the formula he had inherited for this purpose and no alternative presented itself to his mind. The poetry of Homer and Hesiod is full of such traditional expressions.

Another feature of oral poetry is its use of parataxis. The sentences are often long, a succession of coordinated clauses, one idea being added to another like beads on a string. This is a poetry of "and" upon "and."

Two other features typical of oral poetry, though not unique to it, are ring-composition and composition by association of ideas. In order to round off and bring a topic to completion,

the poet often reverts to the idea with which he began, thus
creating a ring-composition. A good example of this occurs in
the description of the Underworld in *Theog.*, where lines 807–
810 repeat lines 736–39 verbatim. Walcot has pointed out that
the main framework of *Theog.* is structured according to a
similar principle.[13] The centerpiece is the story of Prometheus
and the creation of woman. This is preceded by a pair of com-
parable stories: that of the castration of Ouranos by Kronos
and that of the thwarting of Kronos by Zeus; and it is followed
by another pair of comparable stories: that of the war with the
Titans and that of the fight with Typhoeus. Moreover, the
genealogical information between the former pair of stories is
balanced by the description of the Underworld between the
latter pair.

Composition by association of ideas is frequent in *Theog.*,
but it seems even more important for our understanding of
W.D. An oral poet must have begun a poem by getting in
mind what West calls a prospect of his subject, but it is diffi-
cult to imagine that this prospect was very clear to Hesiod
when he first began to compose *W.D.*[14] He probably knew
that he wanted to instruct Perses on justice and the need to
work, and he probably had at his command a number of
proverbs and stories and some valuable information on farm-
ing and perhaps also on sailing, but it seems unlikely that he
had any definite plan for presenting this material. It probably
took him several performances before, by joining one element
to another by an association of ideas, he felt that he had given
his poem a satisfactory form.

Theog. seems to have a more carefully planned structure
than *W.D.*, and we can imagine that Hesiod began it with a
fairly clear prospect of his subject. He knew that he had to
include the Succession Myth and the many catalogs of divini-
ties connected with it. The *Theog.* we have is no doubt the
result of many earlier versions, but the basic outline was prob-
ably there from the beginning.

Although the styles of Hesiod and Homer are essentially
the same, it is still possible to detect some differences between
them. Generally speaking, Homer is the better poet, except

perhaps in catalog poetry, an area in which Hesiod excels. The sections of *Theog.* that give a list of names run very smoothly and melodiously. Elsewhere Hesiod's composition often seems awkward and abrupt. This abruptness, however, goes well with the persistence, the driving emphasis—especially noticeable in *W.D.*—with which he hammers home his message. One of the most striking features of Hesiod's style is his repetition of a key word, like "work" (cf. *W.D.* 298ff.); and he frequently brings a passage to an emphatic close by using the device of repetition (cf. *W.D.* 284f.).

THE PRESENT TRANSLATION AND COMMENTARY

The present translation offers an approximation to the dactylic hexameter of the original. I have tried to translate line by line, but sometimes have taken two or more lines as my unit in order to attain a clear and idiomatic English. Moreover, sometimes the thought of the original has been expanded or made explicit where it was only implicit. This is especially so in the case of lines containing a list of names, as in the catalogs of *Theog.;* for instance, an original *Euterpe* (a name connected with "joy") has been translated "joyful Euterpe." But with the exception of such slight liberties I have tried to be as faithful as possible to Hesiod's thought and spirit.

My translation is based on the Oxford text (1970) by Solmsen, the chief difference being that I have omitted only a few lines, on the ground of their representing un-Hesiodic additions: *Theog.* 196, 218f., 768, 774, 1014, and *W.D.* 169. Some other differences are as follows: in *Theog.* 245 *thoe* is taken to be the adjective "swift" instead of the name "Thoe," and *thalie* to mean "Thalia" instead of "and Halia"; *Theog.* 434 is kept in its transmitted position after 433 and not put after 429; in *Theog.* 450 for *met'ekeinen*, "after her," the emendation *met'ekeines*, "with her help," is accepted; in *W.D.* 533 the word for "mortal" is taken with the manuscripts to be a dative singular instead of a nominative plural; *W.D.* 768 is kept in its transmitted position after 767 and not put after 769; and in *W.D.* 817 an emendation supplying the conjunction "and" is accepted.

The reader should be warned that the division of the translation into sections with titles is not to be found in the original text. It seems likely, however, that these divisions in many cases represent the blocks of thought in which Hesiod actually composed and that thus they are helpful in understanding the structure and content of his poems.

A Comment is made at the end of each section. These Comments are intended to clarify points on which the average reader may need help, to describe the structure of the poems, and to indicate features of style. Parallels from the Bible are frequently quoted in order to illustrate similarities between Hesiod and Near Eastern literature. Among the many scholars to whom these Comments are indebted, M. L. West, Walter Marg, and Walter Nicolai deserve special mention.

NOTES

1. M. L. West, *Hesiod: Theogony* (Oxford, 1966), pp. 44f.

2. See J. N. Coldstream, *Geometric Greece* (London, 1977), pp. 200f.

3. See M. Robertson, *A History of Greek Art* (Cambridge, 1975), 1:20, 30f.

4. See P. W. Wallace, "Hesiod and the Valley of the Muses," *Greek, Roman, and Byzantine Studies* 15 (1974):5–24.

5. See C. G. Starr, *The Economic and Social Growth of Early Greece 800–500 B.C.* (New York, 1977), pp. 125f.

6. For translations of these stories see *Ancient Near Eastern Texts*, ed. J. B. Pritchard, 3rd ed. (Princeton, 1969). For summaries and discussion, P. Walcot, *Hesiod and the Near East* (Cardiff, 1966), chaps. 1 and 2; and West, *Theogony*, pp. 18–31.

7. For an interesting discussion of this topic see F. M. Cross, *Canaanite Myth and Hebrew Epic* (Cambridge, Mass. and London, 1973), esp. chap. 6.

8. There are good discussions of this subject in Walcot, *Hesiod and the Near East*, chap. 4; M. L. West, *Hesiod: Works and Days* (Oxford, 1978), pp. 3–15; and R. B. Y. Scott, *The Way of Wisdom in the Old Testament* (New York and London, 1971).

9. Noted by Walcot, *Hesiod and the Near East*, p. 90.

10. On the early Greek idea of justice *(dike)* see H. Lloyd-Jones, *The Justice of Zeus* (Berkeley and London, 1971), chaps. 1 and 2; and

M. W. Dickie, "*Dike* as a Moral Term in Homer and Hesiod,"
Classical Philology 73 (1978):91–101.

11. See M. C. Stokes, "Hesiodic and Milesian Cosmogonies I,"
Phronesis 7 (1962):1–37.

12. See G. P. Edwards, *The Language of Hesiod in its Traditional
Context* (Oxford, 1976).

13. Walcot, *Hesiod and the Near East,* pp. xiif.

14. West, *Works and Days,* pp. 43ff.

Theogony

AN INTRODUCTORY HYMN TO THE MUSES

Let us now begin our singing with the Helikonian Muses,
who are frequenters of Helikon, a mountain high and holy,
as they dance around some spring's dark water on soft feet
and around the sacred altar of the mighty son of Kronos.
5 Having washed their tender bodies in the streams of the
      Permessos
or the spring called Hippokrene or the holy brook Olmeios,
on the topmost part of Helikon they hold their circling
      dances,
beautiful and charming, tripping lightly on their feet.
Descending from this height, their bodies hidden in dense
      air,
10 through the darkness of the night they pass in lovely song,
hymning Zeus who bears the aigis and Queen Hera,
Argive goddess, who walks on sandals made of gold,
and Athena, gray-eyed daughter of the aigis-bearing Zeus,
and Apollo, brilliant Phoibos, and the arrow-showering
      Artemis,
15 and the god who holds and shakes the earth, Poseidon,
Themis the revered and the bright-eyed Aphrodite,

Hebe of the golden crown and glorious Dione,
Leto and Iapetos and clever-minded Kronos,
Eos and great Helios and the shining moon Selene,
20 Gaia and Okeanos, great river, and black Night,
and the awesome body of the other gods immortal.
These are the Muses who once taught Hesiod beautiful song
as he was pasturing his flock in the foothills of holy Mount
          Helikon.
This is the speech with which I was first addressed by these
          goddesses,
25 the Muses who sing on Olympos, the daughters of Zeus of
          the Aigis:
"Shepherds who dwell in the fields, base creatures, disgraces,
          mere bellies,
we know how to tell numerous lies which seem to be
          truthful,
but whenever we wish we know how to utter the full truth."
Thus did they speak, these eloquent daughters of almighty
          Zeus,
30 and they gave me a rod, the shoot of a flowering laurel,
which they had plucked, a marvelous thing, and breathed
          a divine voice
into me to sing of what will be and what was before;
and they bade me to hymn the race of the blessed
          immortals,
and at the start and the end of my song to honor the Muses.
35 But why linger, why stay in this world of oak tree and rock?
Let us rather begin with the Muses who as they sing their
song to Zeus Father give joy to his wonderful mind on
          Olympos,
as they reveal what is and what will be and what was before,
voices harmonious. A single sweet tone melodiously, easily

40 flows from their lips, and the house of their father Zeus the
        Loud Thunderer
    shimmers with joy at the piercing-sweet sound of their
        voices everywhere
    scattered; echoes roll over the peaks of snowy Olympos
    and through the homes of the gods. They with voices
        immortal
    first in their song offer praise to the holy race of the gods
45 from the beginning, those Gaia bore to broad Ouranos and
    those who were born from these, the gods who are givers
        of blessings.
    Secondly, sing they of Zeus, the Father of Gods and of Men,
    and on beginning and ending their song these goddesses
        praise him,
    telling how he is the best of the gods and the greatest in
        strength.
50 Then the race of men and that of strong-bodied giants are
    praised in song giving joy to the mind of Zeus on Olympos
    by the Olympian Muses, the daughters of Zeus of the Aigis.
    In Pieria, when she had mingled with Zeus, son of Kronos,
        their father,
    Mnemosyne (Memory), queen of the slopes of Eleuther,
        bore these
55 powers that make evils forgotten and bring a cessation to
        sorrows.
    Nine nights Zeus of the Counsels came and mingled with
        her,
    mounting the sacred bed apart from the other immortals;
    and when her time had arrived and the changing seasons
        had passed,
    month upon month having waned, the many days come to
        fulfillment,

60 then she bore him nine daughters who are harmonious
          spirits
     thinking only of song and troubling their hearts with this
          only.
     These she bore close to the uppermost peak of snowy
          Olympos,
     where they have their bright dancing circles and glorious
          dwellings.
     Near them the Graces and Himeros (Desire) dwell in
          bountiful
65 feasting, while they, the Muses, dancing and singing with
          lovely
     voices, glorify the special empowerments and characteristics
     of all the immortals, hymning their praises in lovely song.
     Then they went to Olympos, rejoicing in their beautiful
          voices,
     singing and dancing divinely; and everywhere black earth
          resounded,
70 echoing their singing. From under their feet a lovely sound
          rose
     as they went to their father, to him who is king over heaven,
     for he controls the thunder and smoldering bolt of the
          lightning,
     and he has conquered Kronos, his father, and fairly
          apportioned
     to the immortals each of their rights and granted them
          honors.
75 So they were singing, the Muses, who have their homes on
          Olympos,
     all the divine nine daughters begotten by almighty Zeus:
     Klio, joyful Euterpe, Thalia, songful Melpomene,
     dancing Terpsichore, Erato, Polyhymnia, heavenly Ourania,

and Kalliope, who is the most important of all,
80 for she grants her ready attendance to honorable kings.
He to whom these daughters of almighty Zeus are gracious,
every Zeus-nurtured king they look on with favor at birth,
receives from them on his tongue a sweet pouring of
        heavenly dew,
and from his mouth the words flow with gentleness. Then
        the people
85 all look in honor to him interpreting the laws with verdicts
showing straight justice; and he by his smooth and unerring
        speech
swiftly brings even to great disagreements a skillful solution.
Kings are considered wise because whenever their people
need some redress they in assembly see that they gain it
90 easily, using their skill in the art of gentle persuasion.
When they go through the gathering, their people greet
        them like gods with
blandishing reverence, and they are outstanding among the
        assembled.
Such are the holy gifts of the Muses to mortal men,
for by the power of the Muses and far-shooting Apollo
95 men who sing and play on the lyre exist on the earth and
kings are empowered by the Muses and Zeus. Blessed the
        man who is
loved by the Muses; sweet is the voice that flows from his
        mouth.
So if someone is stricken with grief of a recent bereavement
and is torturing his heart with mourning, then if some singer
100 serving the Muses sings of past glory and heroes of old and
tells of the blessed immortals who have their homes on
        Olympos,
swiftly the grief-stricken one is forgetful and remembers

none of his sorrow; quickly the gifts of the Muses divert
    him.
Hail, daughters of Zeus, grant me, I pray, beautiful song.
105 Gloriously hymn the gods, the holy race of immortals,
those whom Gaia bore in union with star-studded Ouranos,
those arising from black Night, those briny Pontos
    produced.
Tell first of all how the gods and Gaia came into being,
and the rivers and Pontos boundless and raging with waves,
110 and the bright-beaming stars and Ouranos stretching above,
and those born to these, the gods who are givers of blessings;
and tell how they divided their wealth and apportioned
    their honors,
and how they first got control of many-valed Olympos.
These things, O Muses, who have your homes on Olympos,
    tell me
115 from the beginning, and what divine power first came into
    being.

COMMENT

Hesiod, in keeping with the early Greek custom of introducing an epic with a hymn to some god, begins Theog. *with a hymn to the Muses. He addresses them first as the Helikonian Muses because Mount Helikon is where they first inspired him. They are pictured as dancing around the altar of Zeus on the top of this mountain after washing themselves in one of its springs, in much the same way no doubt as human girls were accustomed to do. Helikon abounds in springs, the most famous of which is Hippokrene, "Horse Spring," reputedly brought into being by the blow of the hoof of the divine horse Pegasos. When the Muses have finished their dancing, they pass down the mountain singing a theogony in reverse, beginning with Zeus and ending with Night. This is the first of many catalogs in* Theog.

Did the Muses really reveal themselves to Hesiod and inspire him to sing Theog.? *We must remember that we live in a very different world from Hesiod's, and that others in antiquity (such as Moses, Amos, and the Greek poet Archilochos) are said to have had similar experiences. Sensitive souls brought up to believe in the possibility of such experiences may have been able to have them, and their poetry was later proof of their inspiration. Hesiod shows himself to be a true believer in the Muses when he tells us that he dedicated the tripod-cauldron to them; compare* W.D. *655ff.*

Since the Muses inspire Hesiod to speak the truth, Theog. *must give a truthful account of the gods. The assertion that the Muses sometimes speak falsely shows that there are other accounts with which Hesiod disagrees, such as, it seems likely, a version of the Prometheus story in which Zeus was actually tricked by Prometheus.*

Beginning with line 36, we move from the Helikonian to the Olympian Muses, and are told of their birth and how they first went to Olympos. Mnemosyne (Memory) bore them to Zeus in Pieria, a district just north of Mount Olympos. This was probably their original home, for the place where the cult of a god arises is often identified as his birthplace. Zeus came to Mnemosyne's love nine times and so she produced nine daughters. The Graces and Desire, powers of enchantment with whom the Muses are closely associated, live near them in Pieria. Thus Hesiod expresses relationship in geographical instead of genealogical terms, as he also does later in the description of the Underworld.

The names of the Muses, some or even all of which Hesiod may have invented, are expressions of their powers. For instance, Klio means "Glorifier"; Thalia, "The Bountiful One"; Melpomene, "Songstress"; Terpsichore, "Lover of Dancing"; and Kalliope, "She of the Beautiful Voice." We should note that the Muses do not become patrons of separate departments of literature and science until much later. Even Kalliope, whom Hesiod praises as the inspirer of kings, that is, the nobles of his time, shares her power with her sisters.

The Muses are said to inspire two groups of men, poets and kings. Apollo, the god of the lyre, which he plays for the entertainment of the gods on Olympos, helps them with the poets. Zeus,

*the king of the gods, helps them with the kings. Kings are thus
enabled to speak true judgments in a soothing voice, and are simi-
lar to Zeus in that they see to the maintenance of justice and order
in the world. As for the poets, the Muses enable them to cause
mourners to forget their sorrow. The daughters of Memory are
bringers of forgetfulness — a play on words typical of Hesiod.*

*We end with a transition to the main poem. The Muses are
asked to sing* Theog.

THE EARLIEST POWERS: CHAOS, GAIA, EROS, AND NIGHT

The first power to come into being was Chaos. Then arose
    Gaia,

broad-bosomed earth, which serves as the ever-immovable
    base for

all the immortals who dwell on the peaks of snowy Olympos;

and then shadowy Tartaros deep in the wide-wayed earth;

120 and then Eros surpassing every immortal in beauty,

who, a loosener of limbs, brings all immortals and mortals

under his power and makes them unable to think as they
    should.

And out of Chaos black Night and Erebos came into being,

and out of Night then came the brightness of Aither and
    Day,

125 whom she conceived by lying in love and mingling with
    Erebos.

COMMENT

The great chasm of Chaos is the starting point from which Theog.
*moves to the cosmos of Zeus's orderly government of the world.
Night and Erebos arise out of Chaos, and so apparently do Gaia
(with Tartaros) and Eros. Eros has a place among the earliest*

Eros—from an engraving on a bronze mirror of the archaic period in the British Museum; compare Theog. *120–22.*

powers because of his role as the generating force in creation.

Hesiod usually describes all the divinities of one generation before moving on to the next. Thus he gives us Gaia and Night here, then the children of Gaia (126–210) and the children of Night (211–32), and finally the grandchildren of Gaia (233–500). This scheme, however, is broken in the case of certain divinities who are better listed with the first mention of their parents. Thus Aither (the brightness of the upper air) and Day are listed here along with their parents and necessary complements Erebos (the darkness below) and Night. We might note that Sun is not born until later (371) and that therefore, as in Genesis 1, day is not connected with the light of the sun.

THE CHILDREN OF GAIA

Ouranos, Pontos, and the Titans

Gaia first gave birth to him who is equal to her,
star-studded Ouranos, to cover her everywhere over and
be an ever-immovable base for the gods who are blessed.
And she bore the high mountains, the charming retreats of
      the goddess
130 nymphs who have their abodes in the wooded glens of the
      mountains.
And without any joy of desirable love she brought forth
Pontos, the exhaustless sea that rages with waves. And then
      she,
when she had bedded with Ouranos, bore him deep-swirling
      Okeanos,
Koios and Krios, Hyperion who passes on high, Iapetos,
135 Theia and Rhea, Themis the righteous, mindful
      Mnemosyne,
gleaming, golden-crowned Phoibe and lovely, motherly
      Tethys.

Then, after these, her last offspring was Kronos, the clever
      deviser,
most to be feared of these children, who hated his vigorous
      father.

COMMENT

*After Gaia has produced of herself Ouranos and Pontos, she bears
the twelve Titans (as they are later named) to Ouranos. We shall
see that Kronos and Iapetos are the only bad Titans. The others
side with the gods in the war with Kronos and his forces and so
are rewarded with positions of honor in Zeus's government. Thus
the Succession Myth, which we know to be of foreign origin, seems
here to be in conflict with a native Greek belief in the goodness
of these earlier powers.*

THE CHILDREN OF GAIA

The Kyklopes and the Hundred-Handers

Then she gave birth to the Kyklopes, creatures of marvelous
      power:
140 thundering Brontes, lightening Steropes, strong-hearted
      Arges,
who are the makers and givers to Zeus of thunder and
      lightning.
These resemble the gods in every respect but one,
that they have only one eye set in their foreheads at
      midpoint;
Kyklopes, "Circle-eyed," this is their name because of their
      having
145 only one circular eye set in their foreheads at midpoint.
What strength they have, what power and skill is shown in
      their works.

Then there are others whom Gaia produced in union with
     Ouranos,
three other children, gigantic and mighty, not to be named:
Kottos, Briareos, and Gyges, creatures excelling in power.
150 Misshapen beings, each of them has one hundred arms that
shoot from his shoulders; each of them has fifty heads
growing out of his shoulders over his powerful limbs.
What mighty, invincible strength they have is shown in
     their huge forms.

COMMENT

*The story of the rise of the Titans is delayed in order to describe
the birth of the Kyklopes and the Hundred-Handers, who are also
children of Gaia and Ouranos. They, unlike the Titans, will not
be released from the womb of Gaia when Kronos castrates Ouranos.
They must wait until Zeus rises to power. It is evident that the
description of the Hundred-Handers closely parallels that of the
Kyklopes. This parallelism is continued in* Theog. *by the similar
roles they play as helpers of Zeus.*

The names of Hesiod's Kyklopes are Brontes (from bronte, *"thun-
der"), Steropes (from* sterope, *"lightning"), and Arges (from* arges,
*"bright," an epithet of the thunderbolt). They are divine craftsmen,
thunderbolt-fashioning smiths, who are not to be confused with
Homer's impious shepherds.*

*Of the names of the Hundred-Handers only Briareos, "The Strong
One," seems Greek; but perhaps Hesiod connected Gyges with* guia,
"limbs," and Kottos with kotos, *"rancor."*

THE CHILDREN OF GAIA

*Kronos Castrates Ouranos: The Rise of the Titans
and the Birth of Aphrodite*

All the offspring whom Gaia produced in union with
     Ouranos

155 being the most fearsome of children, their father was driven
        to hate them
    from the beginning. So he hid them away, each one,
    as they came into being, and let them not rise to the light
        from
    down in the hollow of earth; and this was an evil activity
    pleasing to Ouranos. But huge Gaia was groaning within
        and
160 feeling constrained, and so she contrived an evil device.
    Swiftly producing a new kind of metal, gray adamant, she
    created of it a great sickle, and this she displayed to her
        children
    while with pain in her heart she spoke to encourage their
        boldness:
    "Children, my children, whose father is evil, if you will
        follow
165 as I advise you, we shall avenge this wicked dishonor
    done by your father, who was the first to devise the
        unseemly."
    Thus she spoke and all were afraid and none of them
        answered;
    but great Kronos, the clever deviser, feeling emboldened,
    quickly responded and spoke to his dear mother Gaia as
        follows:
170 "Mother, I promise to accomplish this deed and I shall bring
        my
    word to fulfillment, having no care for this father of bad
        name,
    though he is ours, for he was the first to devise the
        unseemly."
    Thus he spoke and greatly delighted the heart of huge Gaia.
    She had him hide himself in an ambush and, putting the
        jagged-toothed

175 sickle into his hands, told him all her deceit.
     So when, bringing on night, great Ouranos came and lay on
     Gaia, desiring her love, closely embracing her, stretching
     everywhere over, then his son from where he was hiding
     stretched out his left hand, and with his right hand wielding
          the sickle,
180 jagged and long, quickly cut off his own father's
     genital parts. Backwards he threw them so that they went
     flying behind him—nor did they go in vain from his hand.
     All the numerous drops of blood that were scattered
     fell upon Gaia, who when the seasons had circled produced
185 the mighty Erinyes (the Furies), and the great-bodied giants
     dressed in resplendent armor and holding long spears in
          their hands,
     and the nymphs they call Melian all over the boundless
          earth.
     As for the genital parts which he had cut off with the
          adamant
     sickle and thrown out into the boisterous sea, they were
190 carried for a long time over the water. Then shining white
          aphros,
     "foam," arose from the flesh of the god, and in this a girl
     came into being. First she approached holy Kythera;
     then, as she moved farther on, she came to sea-girt Kypros,
     where she emerged a revered and beautiful goddess, around
          whose
195 delicate feet the grass grew spontaneously. Gods and men
     call her by various names: Aphrodite because she
     came from the *aphros;* Kythereia because she touched on
          Kythera;
     Kyprogenes because she was born on sea-girt Kypros;
200 and Philommedes because she arose from the *medea,*
          "genitals."

She was attended by Eros and by Himeros (Desire)
from the time of her birth when she went to live with the
gods.
From the beginning she was allotted both among mortals
and the immortals the following portion, and these were her
honors:
205 flirtatious conversations of maidens, smiles and deceits,
sweet delight and passion of love and gentle enticements.
As for the Titans, this was the name that their father, great
Ouranos,
gave as a taunt to them, the children whom he had sired.
"Straining," *titainontes,* he said, they had committed a
terrible,
210 criminal act, and *tisis,* "vengeance," was destined to follow.

COMMENT

The Succession Myth begins in this section. Kronos castrates Ouranos. His throwing the genitals behind him reminds us of the story of Deukalion and Pyrrha, who create men and women by throwing stones over their shoulders.

*Gaia produces three groups of offspring from the blood of Ouranos: the Erinyes, the giants, and the Melian nymphs. The Erinyes are spirits of vengeance who especially uphold the rights of parents against their children. They are thus very appropriately brought forth here; the blood of Ouranos, as it were, cries from the earth for vengeance. The giants pop up fully armed, like the men whom Kadmos and Iason (Jason) bring into being by sowing the earth with dragon's teeth. The Melian nymphs were later identified as female spirits of ash trees (*melie, "ash tree"*), the wood of which was used in the making of spear shafts.*

Aphrodite arises from the genitals of Ouranos that fall in the sea. She probably originated as a Near Eastern goddess, the Greek equivalent of the Phoenician Astarte. Perhaps she owes her connection with the sea to the seafaring Phoenicians. In other authors she is the daughter of Zeus and Dione or of Zeus and Hera. But Hesiod puts her among the pre-Olympians, love being for him one

of the earliest powers. The description of her birth has a hymnic
structure similar to that of the birth of the Muses (53ff.). We
are told her names, how she goes with her attendants to join the
other gods, and what her special powers are. Hesiod explains her
name Philommedes as "genital-loving," but it seems likely that he
also knows the more usual meaning of this word, "smile-loving,"
for he lists meidemata, *"smiles," among the expressions of love*
under Aphrodite's control. We thus have a double etymology similar
to that which he gives for the word Titans.

Ouranos calls his children Titans, which is connected by a double
etymology with titainontes, *"straining," and* tisis, *"retribution."*
Perhaps the straining refers to Kronos's stretching out his hand
to castrate Ouranos. The connection with retribution prepares us
for the next stage in the Succession Myth, when Ouranos's avenging
grandson Zeus will rise to power.

THE PROGENY OF NIGHT

Night bore stygian Moros and black Ker, the spirit of death,
Thanatos (Death) and Hypnos (Sleep) and the race of
      Dreams.
Then, after these, dark Night, a goddess not lying with
      anyone,
brought forth Momos, the spirit of blame, and burdensome
      Misery,
215 and the Hesperides, who over glorious Okeanos guard
the beautiful apples of gold and the trees producing this
      fruit.
And she bore the Moirai and Keres, avengers of evil,
220 who pursue the transgressions both of men and of gods,
never relenting until as demons of terrible wrath
they have wreaked a dire retribution on whoever sins.
Baneful Night also bore Nemesis, an avenging plague for

mortal men; and then Deceit and Sexual Love and

225 baneful Old Age and Eris (Strife), a hard-hearted demon.

And the stygian Eris produced burdensome Labor

and the curse of Forgetfulness, Hunger, and lachrymose
        Pains,

Conflicts of Battle and Fights and Murders and Killings of
        Men,

Quarrels and Lies and Words and Disputations,

230 Disorderly Government and her accomplice, the power of
        Ruin,

and the oath-god Horkos, who is the greatest plague for

every man on the earth who wilfully swears a false oath.

COMMENT

The children of Night are powers connected with darkness, whether physical or spiritual. The Hesperides, for instance, live in the darkness on the other side of Okeanos near the house of Night, while Momos (Blame) and Misery darken man's spiritual life.

The Moirai (Fates) and the Keres are similar to the Erinyes in that they are avengers of trespasses. I have omitted the description of the Moirai in lines 218f.: "Klotho, Lachesis, Atropos, powers that determine the fates of/mortals at birth and grant them to have both good things and bad." These lines are almost identical to lines 905f., where the Moirai are again being described, but as children of Zeus and Themis; and it seems likely that they have been interpolated into the text here from that source. But the question remains why Hesiod gives the Moirai two different parentages in Theog. *Perhaps, as suggested in the Introduction, he is trying to solve the problem posed by the belief that the Moirai and Zeus are equally responsible for men's fates. But perhaps he is also distinguishing between two different functions of the Moirai. Those who are daughters of Night are avengers of evil, while those who are daughters of Zeus and Themis allot good and bad to men in the nature of things and not as punishments.*

The powers of Deceit and Sexual Love are listed together. We can compare the coupling of deceit and love in the story of the

*creation of woman (Pandora) and in the enumeration of Aphro-
dite's powers (205).*

*Night's last child is the bad Eris (Strife), who in turn has a
number of children, among whom are spirits of killing and, last
but not least, the oath-god Horkos, who punishes perjury (for
more on oaths and perjury see* Theog. *399f. and 780ff., which
deal with Styx; and* W.D. *194, 219, and 282ff.). At the begin-
ning of* W.D. *(11ff.) Hesiod introduces another Eris, the good
spirit of peaceful competition, with whom he contrasts the bad
Eris of the present passage.*

THE DESCENDANTS OF PONTOS

His Children: Nereus, Thaumas, Phorkys, Keto, and Eurybia

Pontos begot as his oldest child unlying and truthful
Nereus, which is the name by which the Old Man is called
235 because he's *nemertes,* "unerring," and gentle, and isn't
     forgetful of
righteousness, but is a knower of just and gentle proposals.
And there are others whom Pontos begot by mingling with
     Gaia:
mighty Thaumas, lordly Phorkys, lovely-cheeked Keto,
and Eurybia, who has an adamant heart in her breast.

COMMENT

*Gaia, who is the mother of Pontos's other children, is also probably
the mother of Nereus. Hesiod emphasizes Nereus's truthfulness by
punning on his name with the adjective* nemertes, *"unerring." The
gentleness of Nereus's speech and his concern for truth and justice
remind us of the Muses' inspiration of the nobles (called "kings" in
the text) acting as judges (81ff.).*

*Hesiod probably connected the name Thaumas with the Greek
word for wonder. The derivation of Phorkys is uncertain; it may*

*come from the name of a fish or from an epithet of the sea meaning
"gray." The name Keto can be connected with the Greek word for
sea monster. Eurybia gets her name from an epithet of sea divini-
ties meaning "wide-ruling."*

THE DESCENDANTS OF PONTOS

The Daughters of Nereus

240 Nereus begot a numerous progeny, goddesses all,
borne to him in the exhaustless sea by lovely-haired Doris,
the daughter of Okeanos, the river that flows in unending
     completion:
Protho, Eukrante, Sao the savioress, Amphitrite,
Thetis, Eudora, peaceful Galene, sea-green Glauke,

245 Kymothoe, Speio the swift one, beautiful Thalia,
holy Pasithea, Erato, Eunike, a rosy-armed goddess,
charming Melite, protecting Eulimine, noble Agaue,
Doto the giver and Proto, Pherousa, mighty Dynamene,
isle-haunting Nesaia, shore-haunting Aktaia, Protomedeia,

250 bountiful Doris, Panope, beautiful Galateia,
and the lovely Hippothoe, Hipponoe, rosy-armed goddess,
and Kymodoke (who with wave-calming Kymatolege and
fair-ankled Amphitrite easily gentles the waves on
the misty face of the sea and the blasts of the raging winds),
     and

255 Kymo, Eione, and lovely-crowned Halimede,
and the smile-loving goddess Glaukonome, Pontoporeia,
and Leiagore and Euagore, Laomedeia,
knowing Poulynoe, thoughtful Autonoe, Lysianassa,
buxom Euarne, a shapely and very beautiful girl,

260 Psamathe, graceful nymph of the strand, goddess Menippe,

Neso, Eupompe, righteous Themisto, provident Pronoe,
and Nemertes possessing the mind of her father immortal.
These, then, are the daughters who were begotten by
        blameless Nereus,
fifty daughters in all, knowers of blameless works.

COMMENT

The Nereids are fifty beautiful girls who live in the sea near the
shore and bestow blessings on men. They remind us of the Muses
and the Okeanids. One of them is named Erato, "Lovely One,"
like one of the Muses; another Eudora, "Giver of Good," like one
of the Okeanids; and their mother Doris, after whom one of them
is named, is an Okeanid.

Their names suggest that they preside over two main areas, the
sea and the councils of men. The latter group, which is distinguished
by being listed last, take after their father in that they are gentle
speakers concerned with justice and truth. Most significant are
Leiagore and Euagore, whose names I interpret with Marg to
mean "Gentle in Speech" and "Good in Speech"; and Themisto,
"Righteousness"; Pronoe, "Foresight"; and Nemertes, "The Unerr-
ing One," whose name is derived from the adjective used in line
235 to describe her father.

Hesiod seems very close to imagining the state as a ship, a meta-
phor first found in Alkaios. Vergil is much in the spirit of Hesiod
when in Aeneid *1.142ff. he describes Neptune, with the help of*
Triton and one of the Nereids, calming the storm, and compares
him to an orator bringing a rioting mob under control.

THE DESCENDANTS OF PONTOS

The Children of Thaumas

265 Thaumas took as his wife the daughter of deep-swirling
        Okeanos,
    shining Elektra, and she gave birth to Iris, the swift one,

and the lovely-haired Harpies, Aello and Okypete,
who contend with the blasts of the winds and the birds as they
    fly on
wings that are swift; rapidly do they swoop from on high.

COMMENT

*Thaumas ("Wonder") and Elektra ("Shining") are fitting parents
for bright divinities that strike men with wonder: the rainbow Iris
and the winds Aello ("Whirlwind") and Okypete ("Swift to At-
tack"), called Harpies ("Snatchers") probably because they snatch
men off the face of the sea. The idea of brightness is closely asso-
ciated with that of swiftness, which is another characteristic of
both Iris and the Harpies. Hesiod apparently thinks of their swift-
ness as an inheritance from their grandfather, Okeanos, for the
adjective okus, "swift," which appears in the first part of the
name Okypete and is used of Iris and the wings of the Harpies,
can be thought of (wrongly) as also appearing in the first part of
the name Okeanos.*

THE DESCENDANTS OF PONTOS

The Progeny of Phorkys and Keto: The Monsters

270 Then Keto, mating with Phorkys, produced the lovely-
    cheeked Graiai,
who were gray-haired from birth and so are called by the
    name of
Graiai both by gods immortal and earth-going men:
beautifully gowned Pemphredo, Enyo in gown of bright
    saffron.
And she gave birth to the Gorgons, who dwell across glorious
    Okeanos
275 at earth's end near Night and the beautifully singing
    Hesperides:

Sthenno, Euryale, and she who grievously suffered, Medusa.
She (Medusa) was mortal, they (the other two Gorgons)
immortal and ageless. He of the Black Mane lay with Medusa,
in a soft meadow reclining, in blossoming flowers of the spring,
280 so that when Perseus came and cut off her head from her body
out of her mighty Chrysaor leaped and the horse we call
        Pegasos.
Pegasos was named from his birth by the *pegai*, the "streams,"
        of Okeanos,
Chrysaor from the *aor chryseion*, the "gold sword," he wielded.
Pegasos, leaving the earth, the mother of flocks, flew off and
285 went to the gods, and there he dwells in the palace of Zeus and
brings the bolts of thunder and lightning to Zeus of the
        Counsels.
And Chrysaor begot the three-headed creature named Geryon
on Kallirhoe, who is a daughter of glorious Okeanos.
Geryon it was whom the mighty strength of Herakles slew
290 by his shambling cattle off in the isle Erytheia
on that day when Herakles drove those broad-faced cattle
back to sacred Tiryns; going over Okeanos,
there he slew both Orthos and the herdsman Eurytion
in that shadowy steading far over glorious Okeanos.
295 And she gave birth to another uncontrollable monster,
who in no way resembles either immortals or mortals,
in a great hollow cave: the divine and powerful Echidna,
who is a creature half girl, a glancing-eyed, lovely-cheeked girl,
half a serpent of monstrous size, frightening, enormous,
300 flashing, an eater of raw flesh, under the holy earth.
There is her hollow below, her cave down under the rock,
far away from gods immortal and mortal men;
there have the gods apportioned to her her glorious palace;

baneful Echidna dwells below in the land of the Arimoi,
305 being a nymph immortal and ageless all of her days.
And they say that Typhaon mingled with her in love,
he who is frightening, evil, and lawless with her of the bright
          eyes,
and that having conceived she bore him powerful children.
First she produced the dog Orthos to serve as Geryon's helper.
310 Then she gave birth to one uncontrollable, not to be
          mentioned:
Kerberos, a feeder on raw flesh, Hades' brazen-voiced dog,
who is possessed of fifty heads and is shameless and mighty.
The third child of Echidna was Hydra, a pain-devising
          monster,
Hydra of Lerna, whom Hera, the goddess with white arms,
          reared
315 out of her unappeasable anger at Herakles' strength—but
Hydra was slain with the pitiless bronze by Zeus's son
          Herakles,
the heir of Amphitryon; stalwart Iolaos assisted him,
and Athena, the driver of spoils, gave him her counsels.
And she gave birth to Chimaira, the breather of fire irresistible,
320 who was a creature frightening and huge, swift-footed and
          mighty,
and possessed of three heads: that of a fierce-eyed lion,
that of a she goat *(chimaira)*, and that of a powerful serpent;
in front a lion, a serpent behind, in the middle a she goat,
she breathed forth the frightening strength of blazing fire.
325 Valiant Bellerophon slew Chimaira with Pegasos's help.
And, when she had mated with Orthos, she bore him baneful
Phix, the Thebans' destroyer, and also the lion of Nemea,
who was reared by Hera, the glorious consort of Zeus, and

placed in the hills of Nemea to be a plague unto men.
330 There he dwelled and cheated the race of men of their lives,
lording it over the area of Nemea, Tretos, and Apesas,
but he was brought to submission by powerful Herakles'
      strength.
Keto's last child, her youngest, by mingling in love with
      Phorkys,
was the terrible serpent who lives in a lair of the dark earth
335 out at the world's farthest limits and guards the apples of gold.
These, then, are all the monsters whom Keto and Phorkys
      produced.

COMMENT

*It is not clear who the mothers of Echidna, Chimaira, and Phix
and the Nemean lion are, but I think that the following outline
of the genealogy of the monsters (based on E. Siegmann,* Hermes
*96 [1968], 755f.) probably ascribes them correctly. Keto is the
mother of Echidna and Chimaira, and Chimaira is the mother of
Phix and the Nemean lion. There are four lines of descent from
Keto and Phorkys:*

*First that of the Graiai and the Gorgons. One of the Gorgons,
Medusa, gives birth by Poseidon (He of the Black Mane) to
Pegasos and Chrysaor; and Chrysaor begets Geryon.*

*Second that of Echidna. She gives birth by Typhaon (an alternate
form of Typhoeus) to Orthos, Kerberos, and Hydra.*

*Third that of Chimaira. She gives birth by Orthos to Phix (an
alternate form of Sphinx) and the Nemean lion.*

*Fourth that of the serpent who guards the golden apples of the
Hesperides.*

*The first three lines of descent end with the description of a
labor of Herakles in which a monster is slain; and the last reminds
us of another of his labors, that of bringing back the golden apples*

of the Hesperides. Hesiod probably omits this labor because its per-
formance did not entail the slaying of the serpent who guards the
apples. The mention of the serpent and the apples at the end of the
catalog of monsters looks back to the mention of the Hesperides at
its beginning (275), thus enclosing this section in a neat ring-
composition.

We are told of three monster-slayers, Herakles, Perseus, and
Bellerophon, by far the most famous of whom is Herakles. Later
in Theog., Zeus even allows him to slay the eagle that preys on
the liver of Prometheus (526–33).

Although Hesiod does not describe the death of Phix (Sphinx),
his audience probably knew the story of her fatal encounter with
Oidipous. But in the earliest version of this story, to which Hesiod
may be alluding, Oidipous may have slain her in combat instead
of forcing her to commit suicide by solving her riddle.

The monsters tend to live in the far west across Okeanos where
the Underworld begins (the idea that the far west, the place of the
setting sun, is where the Underworld begins is found in Egyptian
literature of a very early date). But monsters can also live in caves
on the earth, which are thought of as leading into the world below.
Thus we are asked to imagine Echidna gloriously housed in a hollow
somewhere under the earth, probably in Asia Minor.

We know that Greek stories about monster-slayers owe a great
deal to Near Eastern mythology. .The Near East, which was the
great breeding ground of the composite monster, gave birth to Chi-
maira, Sphinx, Echidna, and Typhoeus. The idea of the sphinx
seems to have come to Greece from Egypt by way of Phoenicia,
for the original Egyptian one has a wingless lion's body and the
head of a man (the pharaoh), while later Phoenician ones resemble
the Greek Sphinx in having winged Lion's bodies and women's
heads.

The monster-slayers of the present section foreshadow Zeus as the
slayer of Typhoeus. Just as Hera rears Hydra and the Nemean lion
to test the strength of Herakles, so Gaia will produce Typhoeus to
be the last enemy of Zeus.

BENEFICENT TITANIC POWERS

The Children of Okeanos and Tethys

Tethys bore to Okeanos the rivers that swirl in their courses:
Nile and Alpheios and deep Eridanos swirling with eddies,
Strymon, Maiander, and Ister flowing with beautiful waters,
340 Phasis and Rhesos, Acheloos the silvery swirler,
Nessos and Rhodios, salt-rich Haliakmon, and the
           Heptaporos,
then the Granikos and the Aisepos, divine Simois,
and the Peneios and Hermos, the beautifully flowing Kaikos,
and the mighty Sangarios, Ladon and the Parthenios,
345 and the Euenos and the Ladeskos and godlike Skamander.
And she bore daughters, a race that is holy, who over the
           earth,
helped by lordly Apollo and by the rivers, act as
nurses to men, for Zeus has granted this office to them:
Peitho, a nymph of persuasion, Admete, Ianthe, Elektra,
350 Doris, Prymno who dwells in the foothills, godlike Ourania,
Hippo and Klymene, rosy Rhodeia, lovely Kallirhoe,
Zeuxo, Klytie, knowing Idyia, nimble Pasithoe,
splashing Plexaura and bright Galaxaura and lovely Dione,
Melobosis, swift Thoe, shapely Polydora,
355 and Kerkeis, a beautiful girl, and the soft-eyed Pluto,
and Perseis, Ianeira, Akaste, and Xanthe,
lovely, rock-haunting Petraia, steady Menestho, Europa,
Metis the wise one, lawful Eurynome, bright-robed Telesto,
and the golden Chryseia and Asia and charming Kalypso,
360 and Eudora and Tyche, Amphirho, Okyrhoe, and finally
Styx, the water of hate, the most revered of them all.
These are the most illustrious daughters of all those produced
           by
Okeanos and Tethys, but there are many others besides them,

for there are three thousand daughters of Okeanos, trim-
        ankled girls,

365 scattered abroad on the earth and dwelling in the depths of
        the water,

everywhere showing their power, glorious children divine.

No less numerous than these are those others, the rivers that
        roar,

who are the sons whom her majesty Tethys produced with
        Okeanos.

Hard would it be for one mortal to tell all the names of these
        sons,

370 but everyone everywhere knows the river he happens to
        live by.

COMMENT

*Okeanos and Tethys have as their sons the rivers and as their
daughters the springs. Hesiod gives us the names of only twenty-
five rivers, beginning with the Nile, the great river of Egypt,
and ending with the Skamander, the famous river of Troy. Most
of these rivers can be located in the east, in Greece or Asia Minor
or along the coast of the Black Sea. The Hermos and the Kaikos,
for instance, are near Kyme, in Asia Minor, the town from which
Hesiod's father originally came; and the Ister can be identified with
the Danube. Only the Eridanos, perhaps to be identified with the
Po, perhaps with the Rhone, belongs in the west.*

*The catalog of springs begins with a sentence on the function of
springs (and also of rivers) in the government of Zeus: they (along
with Apollo and the rivers) are nurses of men. Perhaps Hesiod
connected Tethys, their mother's name, with* tithene, *"nurse."
Two or more divinities often work together in the performance of
a single service. Just as Apollo helps the Muses to inspire poets
(94ff.), so he helps the rivers and springs to rear the young. Rivers
and springs are easy to imagine as life-giving nurses, for they flow
through the land bringing nourishment to fields, flocks, and men.*

Hesiod lists forty-one springs, the last one being Styx, the most important of all. Later in Theog., *Styx and her children are the first to side with Zeus against the Titans (383ff.), and we are told how her water is used in the oath of the gods (790ff.). Many of the springs have names that show them to be suitable nurses, such as Peitho, "The Persuader"; Doris, "The Giver"; Polydora, "Giver of Many Things"; Eudora, "Giver of Good Things"; Idyia, "The Knowing One"; Metis, "The Wise One"; and Tyche, "Fortune." Closely connected with these are Melobosis, "Flock Tender"; and Pluto, "Wealth Bringer." Others have names that show them to be beautiful girls or swift and bright spirits of the water. We should note that the names Europa and Asia are not connected in Hesiod with continents, and that Kalypso, "The Concealer," perhaps so called because she flows for part of her course under the earth, is not the famous nymph of the* Odyssey. *Okyrhoe, "She Who Flows Swiftly," is the next to the last to be listed, and her name apparently echoes that of her father, Okeanos, in the same way as Nemertes, the last to be named of the Nereids, does Nereus.*

Okeanids make excellent wives. As we have already seen, Doris is married to Nereus (241), Elektra to Thaumas (266), and Kallirhoe to Chrysaor (288). Later we shall find that Metis and Eurynome are married to Zeus (886 and 907), and that Perseis is married to Helios (957) and Idyia to Aietes (960).

BENEFICENT TITANIC POWERS

The Children of Hyperion and Theia

Theia gave birth to mighty Helios and beaming Selene and
Eos the bright one, who shines for every mortal on earth
and for the immortal gods who dwell in broad heaven above;
these were her children when she had yielded in love to

     Hyperion.

COMMENT

Helios (Sun), Selene (Moon), and Eos (Dawn) are a natural three-some. As we have already seen in the case of the Kyklopes, the

Hundred-Handers, and the children of Thaumas and Elektra,
Hesiod likes triads. As an early riser, he seems to have felt a
special reverence for Dawn, whom he praises in W.D. 578ff. for
starting the farmer on his work.

BENEFICENT TITANIC POWERS

The Descendants of Krios and Eurybia. Styx and Her Children

375 And Eurybia, a goddess divine, when she had mingled with
Krios in love, bore him mighty Astraios, Pallas, and
Perses, who is a power surpassing all others in wisdom.
And Eos bore to Astraios the winds who are mighty in spirit,
sky-clearing Zephyros, swiftly moving Boreas, and Notos;
380 these she, a goddess, produced, having lain in love with a god.
Then, after these, the Early Born bore the star named
        Eosphoros
and the sparkling stars with which high heaven is crowned.
And Styx, the daughter of Okeanos, mingling with Pallas,
        produced
Zelos and beautiful-ankled Nike at home in her palace;
385 and she gave birth to Kratos and Bia, glorious children.
Theirs is no house which is far off from Zeus, nor have they
        a seat nor
make they a journey unless they are following this god as their
        leader,
but they are always seated beside loud-thundering Zeus.
So Styx arranged it, the unfailing daughter of Okeanos,
390 when the Olympian One, Zeus, the Lord of the Lightning,
        having
summoned all the immortal gods to lofty Olympos,
promised not to deprive of his power any god who would give
        him
aid in the war with the Titans, but that each one would retain
whatever earlier honor he had among the immortals;
395 as for those who were lacking in honor and power under
        Kronos,

these would then enter on honor and power, as would be
        right.

Then the unfailing Styx, following her father's advice, was
first to come to Olympos, bringing her children along.

So she was granted by Zeus honor and gifts in abundance,

400 for he established her water for use in the gods' mighty oath
        and

made her children to be dwellers forever with him.

Thus in like manner for all he exactly brought to fulfillment

what he had promised, and his is the great power, his is the
        kingship.

COMMENT

Eurybia and Krios produce the triad of Astraios, Pallas, and Perses. Perses, who is praised for his wisdom, becomes (in the next section) the father of the great goddess Hekate. Perhaps Hesiod's brother was named after him in the hope—proved false in the event—that he would turn out to be wise.

Eos (Dawn), who is called the Early Born, and Astraios ("The Starry One") produce the triad of winds and also the stars. Among the stars Eosphoros, the dawn or morning star, the brightest of them all, receives special mention. Hesiod was probably unaware that the morning and evening stars are the same planet (Venus). Perhaps the three winds are related to Eos and Eosphoros because they start blowing at dawn. The north wind Boreas is associated with winter, the west wind Zephyros with summer, and the south wind Notos with autumn; compare W.D. 506ff., 594, and 675. In Theog. 870 these winds are distinguished from the wild winds that arise from the defeated Typhoeus.

The children of Styx by Pallas are Zelos (the spirit of Zeal in the Vindication of one's rights), Nike (Victory), Kratos (Sovereignty), and Bia (Power). Perhaps the name of their father, Pallas, can be connected with the verb pallo, *"brandish," in the sense of brandishing a spear, which would suit their warlike character. We are told, in a narrative that refers to the beginning of the war with the*

Titans *(a part of the Succession Myth), how they became the constant companions of Zeus. Their attendance upon him reminds us of the description of God in Psalm 96:6: "Majesty and splendor attend him, might and beauty are in his sanctuary."*

The gods swear by the water of Styx, whose name, being connected with the verb "hate," shows that she is hateful to them. This oath is a reflection of oaths among men, for men were accustomed to swear by the water of springs, whose subterranean depths were thought to house divinities capable of punishing perjury. In Theog. 780ff. we are given a description of the oath by Styx and of the punishment that false-swearing gods are forced to endure.

BENEFICENT TITANIC POWERS

The Descendants of Koios and Phoibe. The Great Goddess Hekate

Then bright Phoibe came to Koios's much-desired bed
405 and conceiving, a goddess lying in love with a god,
bore him black-robed Leto, who is gentle forever,
being kindly disposed both to immortals and mortals,
one who was gentle from the beginning, the kindest Olympian.
And she gave birth to Asteria of good name, who was by Perses
410 led to his great house that she might be acclaimed as his dear
          wife.
And she, Asteria, conceiving bore Hekate, who more than all
          others was
honored by Zeus, son of Kronos: he gave her glorious rights,
so that she shares in the powers of the earth and the exhaustless
          sea;
and she also shares in the honors of star-studded heaven;
415 and she is held especially in honor among the immortals.
Such are her powers, for now when any man living on earth,
making beautiful sacrifice, prays with ritual due, he

calls upon Hekate; and great is the honor he very easily
gains if only this goddess propitiously answers his prayer and
420 grants him a blessed existence, for she possesses such power.
She has a share in the power of every immortal who,
being descended from Gaia and Ouranos, came into honor.
Nor did Zeus, son of Kronos, constrain her nor take away any
right which was hers among the earlier gods, the Titans,
425 but she has just what she got when the first division was made.
Nor in view of the fact that she was an only child
did she obtain less honor on earth or in heaven or sea,
but much more than before, for Zeus has granted her honor.
She is abundantly present to bless whomever she wills to.
430 He whom she wills to be eminent stands out in the people's
                assembly;
    and when they've put on their armor and gone into man-
                slaying war,
    there is this goddess at hand for men on whom she is willing
    graciously to bestow victory, granting superior power;
    and in decisions of justice she sits by the honorable kings.
435 Good is she too whenever the athletes compete in the games,
    where for whomever this goddess is present, granting him aid,
    he, by his force and strength being victor, easily, joyfully
    wins the beautiful prize and gives delight to his parents;
    and she is good to stand by the charioteer whom she wills to.
440 And for those who are working the boisterous, dark-blue sea
                and
    call upon Hekate and the loud-roaring Shaker of Earth,
    easily does she, a glorious goddess, grant them a large catch or
    easily take one away that seemed likely, should she so will to.
    And she is good in the stables with Hermes to bring the stock
                increase:
445 herds of cattle, flocks of goats that spread out to feed, and

flocks of sheep with their deep wooly fleeces, should she so
    will it,

grow from a few to be many or fall off from many to few.

So in spite of her being the only child of her mother,

honor and power are vouchsafed to her among all the
    immortals.

450 And Zeus made her a nurse of the young, who having her aid
    were

able to see the light which the far-seeing dawn emits.

So from the first she was nurse of the young, and these were
    her honors.

COMMENT

*Phoibe and Koios produce two daughters, Leto and Asteria. Leto
is later described as the mother of Apollo and Artemis (918–20),
but here she is praised entirely on her own account as the gentlest
and kindest of all divinities. Asteria, "The Starry One," an appro-
priate daughter for Phoibe, "The Bright One," is the mother by
Perses of the great goddess Hekate. Hesiod apparently thinks of
Hekate as inheriting the brightness of her mother and the wisdom
of her father (377). He rejects the idea of her as a goddess con-
nected mainly with the Underworld and worshipped especially by
witches.*

*Hekate is described as sharing in the powers of all the other
gods and goddesses, whether of heaven, earth, or sea. We are re-
minded of the fact that two or more divinities often share in the
performance of the same activity. Zeus, after the defeat of the
Titans, confirms her in all her earlier rights—a theme we saw in
the passage on Styx and her children—and even adds to these. We
are twice told that she is an only child. This shows her uniqueness,
but it also seems to mean that since she has no brothers she must
depend on Zeus to protect her interests. Thus Hesiod is able to
praise her as a universal divinity while at the same time main-
taining the preeminence of Zeus.*

How can we explain Hesiod's glorification of Hekate? She was probably never so important in actual cult as he would have us believe. Perhaps his family was especially devoted to her as a tradition derived from Asia Minor, where her cult seems to have originated. I like the suggestion, for which Marg argues, that Hesiod connects her name with the participle hekon, *"being willing," and the preposition* hekati, *"by the will of," which is used with the names of gods (see also P. Walcot, "Hesiod's Hymns to the Muses, Aphrodite, Styx and Hecate,"* Symbolae Osloenses *34 [1958], 11). Hekate thus represents the divine will upon which every worshipper must rely in every petition. Any prayer to any divinity is also addressed to her because it is made with the proviso "if god be willing." It must be admitted, however, that the words* hekon *and* hekati *do not appear in our text. But Hesiod repeatedly uses the verb* ethelo, *"will," in such phrases as "whomever she wills to" and "should she so will to." The emphasis on her will is also seen in statements that describe her as being able to do either of two exactly opposite things. She can grant fishermen either a good catch or no catch at all, and can cause the herds and flocks either to increase or decrease; compare* W.D. *2ff. on the will of Zeus.*

Hesiod's praise of Hekate reminds us of the hymn to the Muses at the beginning of Theog. *and of the passage on the birth of Aphrodite. This is especially true of the description of her various functions, a feature typical of hymns. We are finally told, at the end of the list of her functions, that she is a nurse of the young. Thus not even the three thousand rivers and three thousand springs, who are also nurses of the young, are more universal than she is.*

THE RISE OF ZEUS

The Birth of Zeus and the Other Olympians, the Children of Kronos and Rhea

And Rhea, mating with Kronos, bore him glorious children:
Hestia, Demeter, and Hera, who walks on sandals of gold;
455 powerful Hades, who dwells in a mansion under the earth and

has a pitiless heart; the roaring Shaker of Earth; and
Zeus of the Counsels, who is the Father of Gods and of Men
and at the sound of whose thundering a trembling seizes the
> broad earth.
Great Kronos swallowed each of these children as each of
> them came
460 out of the holy womb of their mother and fell at her knees,
this his set purpose, that no other lordly descendant of Ouranos
should possess the honor of kingship among the immortals.
For he had learned of the future from Gaia and star-studded
> Ouranos,
how he was destined to meet with defeat at the hands of his
> son;
465 this was to be in spite of his strength, for great Zeus would
> plan it.
Therefore no blind man's lookout was his, but he being
> watchful
swallowed his children, and Rhea was seized with a grief
> unforgettable.
But when she was finally about to give birth to Zeus,
the Father of Gods and of Men, then she begged her dear
> parents,
470 Gaia and star-studded Ouranos, who were her mother and
> father,
that they should tell her how she might secretly bear her dear
> baby,
and how her father's Erinys might be an avenger against
great Kronos, the clever deviser, in payment for swallowing
> her children.
They then heeded their daughter's request and did as she
> asked them,
475 telling her all that was destined to be, revealing the future,

what was to happen to Kronos the king and her stout-hearted
    son.

And they sent her to Lyktos, off in fertile-soiled Krete,

when she was going to bear him, her youngest, the last of her
    children,

Zeus, great Zeus. There in the broad isle of Krete huge Gaia

480 received him from her in order to nurse him and rear him to
    manhood.

Bringing him there she came in the covering darkness of swift
    night

first to Lyktos, and taking him into her hands she put him

into a cave under the holy earth high up

on Mount Aigaion, where is abundant thickly grown forest.

485 And she swaddled a great stone and put it into the hands of

Ouranos's son, the great lord, king of the earlier gods,

who, having taken it from her, sent it down into his stomach,

hardhearted wretch, nor did he foresee what was going to
    happen,

that his son, replaced by the stone, unconquered and carefree,

490 still surviving, would prove himself victor by force of his
    hands and

drive him out of his honor and rule as king of the gods.

Then the strength and the glorious power of the limbs of this
    king`

rapidly grew and, the circling year having come to completion,

great Kronos, the clever deviser, being the dupe of Gaia's

495 very superior advice, sent up his children again,

for he was brought to defeat by the trickery and force of his
    son.

First he was forced to spew up the stone—he had swallowed
    it last—and

this was established and fixed by Zeus in the wide-wayed
    earth at
holy Pytho down in the hollow beneath Mount Parnassos,
500 there to remain as a sign, a marvel for mortal men.

COMMENT

*Kronos and Rhea produce a triad of females and a triad of males.
The first female, Hestia, the goddess of the hearth, is a vague figure
about whom there is very little mythology. Demeter, the second fe-
male, is the goddess of the grain; she is married to Zeus, by whom
she produces Persephone (912ff.). The third female, Hera, becomes
the last wife of Zeus, by whom she produces Hebe, Ares, and Eilei-
thyia (921ff.).*

*The first male is Hades, the king of the Underworld; his name
is often used to stand for the Underworld itself. The second male,
Poseidon, is the god of the sea and the waters under the earth; he
is called the Shaker of Earth because he sometimes causes earth-
quakes. Zeus, who is the greatest of the gods, surpassing all others
in wisdom and power, holds the last and most important position.
His power is made manifest by his thunderbolts, which he obtains
from the Kyklopes in the next section. With the birth of Zeus,*
Theog. *reaches the goal toward which the preceding sections have
been pointing. From now on he will dominate the stage as he
defeats all his enemies and consolidates his government in the final
events of the Succession Myth.*

*The story of the birth of the gods has several parallels with that
of the birth of the Titans. Kronos and Ouranos both try to suppress
their children and so cause their wives great pain, but finally their
youngest sons take vengeance upon them and drive them from power.
The two stories are closely connected by the theme of vengeance.
We remember that the Erinyes (Furies), who are spirits of ven-
geance, spring up from the blood of Ouranos's castration.*

*Greek civilization was greatly influenced by the earlier Minoan
civilization on Krete (Crete), and the Greek Zeus was identified
with a Minoan god of vegetation who was thought of as dying*

*and being born again every year. Thus Krete became the birthplace
of Zeus. Some Greeks also spoke of a tomb of Zeus on Krete, but
most found this impossible to believe, for Zeus was immortal.
Plutarch (*Moralia *153F) tells how at the funeral games of Am-
phidamas Homer challenged Hesiod with the following words:*

> *Muse, tell me such things as never have happened before and
> never will happen in future.*

To which Hesiod answered:

> *But when horses with clattering hoofs run their course
> around Zeus's tomb and shatter their chariots striving for victory.*

*It was for this answer, Plutarch says, that Hesiod was awarded
the prize of the tripod-cauldron. Although this story is probably
apocryphal, it is a good illustration of the fact that most Greeks,
and certainly Hesiod, believed in the immortality of Zeus. There
never had been and never would be a tomb of Zeus on Krete or
anywhere else. There never would be funeral games, such as the
race with horse and chariot, held in his honor.*

*When Zeus has forced Kronos to spew up the stone along with
his brothers and sisters, he sets it up at Pytho (an ancient name
for Delphi) to be a memorial of his victory. It was a common
practice for victors, whether in war or at the Panhellenic games,
to set up tokens of their victory at Delphi for all the world to see.*

THE RISE OF ZEUS

Zeus Obtains the Kyklopes' Thunderbolts

And he loosed from their terrible bonds his father's brothers,
the children of Ouranos, who in his madness had kept them
      in bondage.
And in return for this kindness they showed themselves
      grateful to him by
giving him both the crash of the thunder and the smoldering
      bolt and

505 flash of the lightning—these until then huge Gaia had
            hidden—
      which are the weapons Zeus uses to rule all immortals and
            mortals.

COMMENT

*It is not clear that this passage is concerned only with the Kyklopes,
and not with the Hundred-Handers as well, until the thunder and
lightning are mentioned. Perhaps this confusion is intentional. The
present section and that in which the Hundred-Handers are freed,
can be thought of as framing the very important next section that
deals with the fate of man and shows that no other power is able
to outsmart Zeus.*

*The thunderbolt, by means of which Zeus will defeat the Titans
and Typhoeus, was for the ancient Greeks a frightening proof of
his power. In later antiquity the philosophers were eager to explain
thunder and lightning as natural phenomena in order to liberate
men from the fear of the gods.*

ZEUS OUTWITS PROMETHEUS

The Maleficent Sons of Iapetos

And Iapetos took as his wife a trim-ankled girl, Klymene,
one of the daughters of Okeanos, and went with her into their
            bed.
And she produced four sons: strong-hearted, enduring Atlas;
510 Menoitios, who was swollen with arrogance; forethoughtful
            Prometheus,
      cunning and devious-minded; and erring-in-thought
            Epimetheus,
      who from the first was an evil for men who are eaters of bread,
      being the first to receive from Zeus, when she had been
            fashioned,

Atlas and Prometheus—from a painting on a vase of the sixth century
B.C. *in the Museo Vaticano. The serpent is no doubt the guardian of the golden apples of the Hesperides, before whom Atlas is said to stand; compare* Theog. *333ff. and 517f. Prometheus is bound to the column at midpoint; compare* Theog. *522.*

woman, the maiden. Hybristic Menoitios was cast into
    Erebos by
515 far-seeing Zeus, who hurled a smoldering bolt against him,
that he might pay for his blindness of heart and towering
    arrogance.
And Atlas is forced to sustain the burden of broad heaven,
standing at earth's end before the clear-voiced Hesperides,
using his head and the weariless power of his arms to support it;
520 this is the fate that Zeus of the Counsels apportioned to him.
And in fast bondage he bound Prometheus, the devious
    planner,
whipping the painful bindings over a column at midpoint,
and against him sent a long-winged eagle to feed on his liver,
which was immortal; but whatever this long-winged bird ate
525 during the day grew during the night again to completion.
This evil plague of a bird was finally slain by Herakles,
the lovely-ankled Alkmene's valiant son, who kept it from
further attacks on Iapetos's son and freed him from pains.
Thus it was willed by Zeus the Olympian, the ruler on high,
530 so that the glory of Herakles, the Theban-born hero's renown,
might be greater than even before on the life-giving earth.
So by this honor Zeus showed his regard for his glorious son,
relenting, though angry still, from his earlier wrath at
    Prometheus's
matching wits with himself, the mighty son of Kronos.

COMMENT

*This passage brings to an end the genealogy of the Titans. Iapetos's
sons are all in some way punished by Zeus. Of special importance
to Hesiod because of their connection with the creation of woman
are Prometheus, "The Forethinker"; and Epimetheus, "The After-
thinker."*

    Prometheus is treated as a very unsympathetic character who is deservedly punished for trying to outwit Zeus. He is bound to a column, and an eagle is sent to feed on his liver. The place of his binding is probably in the Caucasus mountains, and so he is situated out in the east, apparently balancing Atlas who holds up the sky out in the west. Although Zeus permits Herakles to slay the eagle, nothing is said about the release of Prometheus, and, as West points out, Hesiod seems to imagine his bondage as an eternal punishment.

ZEUS OUTWITS PROMETHEUS

The Creation of Woman

535 For when the gods and mortal men fell to disputing
      at Mekone, Prometheus, acting in a spirit of kindness,
      divided and dished up a great ox, deceiving the mind of Zeus.
      On the one side he put the flesh and the rich and fat inner
             parts
      hidden under the skin, concealed in the paunch of the ox;

540 on the other side he put the ox's white bones, arranging them
      well with skillful deception, concealed in silvery fat.
      Then the Father of Gods and of Men addressed him as follows:
      "Son of Iapetos, lord surpassing all others in glory,
      ah my good fellow, how very unfairly you make this division!"

545 Thus did Zeus, whose plans are unfailing, chidingly speak.
      And Prometheus, the clever deviser, made him this answer,
      gently smiling the while and mindful of skillful deception:
      "Zeus, most glorious and greatest of gods eternally living,
      choose for yourself of these helpings the one that your heart
             desires."

550 Thus he spoke with deceit, but Zeus, whose plans are
             unfailing,

saw through the trick and wasn't deceived, but planned in his
    heart
evil which he would bring to fulfillment for mortal men.
Then as in both hands he took up the helping shining with fat
anger swelled in his breast, wrath entered into his heart,
555 for he beheld the white bones of the ox and the skillful
    deception.
(This explains why the tribes of men who dwell on the earth
burn white bones on the fragrant altars to the immortals.)
Then, greatly angered, Zeus of the Storm Cloud addressed
    him as follows:
"Son of Iapetos, you who surpass all others in planning,
560 ah my good fellow, you ever are mindful of skillful deception!"
Thus in his wrath Zeus, whose plans are unfailing, spoke.
And he never forgot this act of deception but thereafter
no longer gave to the ash trees the strength of weariless fire,
which is a boon for mortal men who dwell on the earth.
565 But the goodly son of Iapetos deceived him by thievery,
stealing the strength of weariless fire, that far-shining
    brightness,
caught in a fennel stalk's hollow—a deed that pierced to the
    heart
Zeus the Thunderer on High, stirring his spirit to anger,
when he beheld among men the far-shining brightness of fire.
570 Immediately he made as the price of fire an evil for men,
for the famous Lame-Legged One fashioned of clay,
as Zeus decreed, an image resembling a virgin demure.
And the goddess gray-eyed Athena girdled and dressed her
in a silver-white gown and over her head drew a veil,
575 one that was woven with wonderful skill, a marvel to look at;
and over this a garland of spring flowers, bright in their
    freshness,

Pallas Athena set on her head, a lovely adornment;
and a gold crown, encircling the brow, she put in its place,
which had been made by the famous Lame-Legged One
     himself,
580 using the skill of his hands, gladly obliging Zeus Father.
On it were made many intricate shapes, marvels to look at,
resembling the terrible monsters spawned by earth and sea;
many of these he put there with charm breathing over each one,
marvelous beings which seemed to be living and able to roar.
585 When he had finished this beauty, this evil to balance a good,
Hephaistos brought her among the other gods and men,
glorying in her adornment by the gray-eyed Daughter of
     Great Zeus.
Then the gods and mortal men were struck with amazement
when they beheld this sheer inescapable snare for men.
590 From her descend the race of women, the feminine sex;
from her come the baneful race and types of women.
Women, a great plague, make their abodes with mortal men,
being ill-suited to Poverty's curse but suited to Plenty.
Compare how the honey bees in the protected cells of the hives
595 garner food for the drones, conspirers in evil works—
all day long they are active until the sun goes down
busily working and storing white honey during the daylight—
while the drones keep within the protected cells of the hives
     and
garner into their stomachs the food that the others have
     worked for.
600 Even so Zeus the Thunderer on High created women
as an evil for men and conspirers in troublesome works.
And in exchange for a good he gave a balancing evil.
Whoever flees from marriage and women's mischievous works,
being unwilling to wed, comes to baneful old age with

605 no one to care for his needs, and though he has plenty to live on
     while he is living, collateral heirs divide his possessions
     when he is dead. As for the man who is fated to marry,
     if he obtains a virtuous wife, one endowed with good sense,
     throughout his life evil and good alternate endlessly.
610 But that man who obtains a wife who is thoroughly bad
     lives having deep in his breast a pain which never subsides
     fixed in his innermost heart, and this is an evil incurable.
     Thus to deceive Zeus's mind is impossible or to get round it,
     for not even the son of Iapetos, crafty Prometheus,
615 avoided his deep wrath, but he in spite of his shrewdness
     suffers under compulsion great inescapable bondage.

COMMENT

Prometheus tries to trick Zeus at Mekone (identified with Sikyon, in the Peloponnese) by making him choose the bones instead of the meat. But Hesiod's Zeus (probably contrary to an earlier version) is not tricked; he chooses the bones with the intention of punishing men, for whom Prometheus has gained the meat. This is an aetiological myth used to explain why men obtain the meat of sacrificial victims but the gods only the bones.

Zeus punishes men by taking fire from the ash trees (which are especially good for kindling) and so men are unable to cook the meat. Prometheus counters by stealing fire in a fennel stalk, an appropriate vehicle, for we elsewhere hear of the stalk of the giant fennel being used for carrying fire. This theft results in Zeus's final punishment: woman is sent to man and (though this is not said here) Prometheus is bound and afflicted with the eagle.

Woman is created out of clay by the Lame-Legged One (Hephaistos) and dressed by Athena. Her last adornment is a crown made by Hephaistos showing representations of monstrous animals. Hesiod's remark on the very lifelike appearance of these animals is inconsistent with the fact that the art of his time was highly stylized. As Marg notes, it was an old, naïve way of praising a work of art, found also in Homer (Iliad 18.478ff.) and often in later Greek literature, to say that its representations were lifelike.

Women are an economic burden, that is, drones. Compare W.D. 302ff., where lazy men are equated with drones. Moreover, the creation of woman raises the problem of marriage, and this problem shows how the lives of men are circumscribed by fate.

A man will have a mixed life of good and bad whether he refuses to marry or even if, choosing to marry, he obtains a good wife. But if he chooses to marry and finds a bad wife, he will have an entirely bad life. These are the only two kinds of life available to him. This view of man's fate seems to have been common in Hesiod's time as well as in later Greek history. As noted in the Introduction, it occurs in the description of the jars of Zeus in Iliad 24.525ff.

The moral of the whole Prometheus story is that no one is able to deceive Zeus. A similar idea is expressed in Proverbs 19:21: "A man's heart may be full of schemes, but the Lord's purpose will prevail." The present passage should be compared with that on the creation of Pandora in W.D. 42–105, which ends with the same moral. There man's fate is explained by Pandora's opening of a great jar of evils.

THE WAR WITH THE TITANS

Zeus Obtains the Hundred-Handers' Assistance

Since from the first their father Ouranos was angry at heart with
Briareos, Kottos, and Gyges, he bound them in bondage
    secure,
  for their overpowering strength, the shapes of their bodies,
    their hugeness
620 held him in awe; he kept them under the wide-wayed earth,
sitting at earth's end, at the great earth's ultimate limits,
  being for a long time in much anguish, having great grief in
    their hearts.
But then Zeus, son of Kronos, and the other immortal gods

625 whom the lovely-haired Rhea bore of her union with Kronos,
     following Gaia's advice, led them back to the light,
       for she had told them all that would happen, the course of
              events,
       how with these aiding them they would win victory and
              glorious fame.
       Now for a long time they had been fighting in heart-rending
              battle,
630 coming against each other in mighty encounters of war,
     they the immortal Titans and they who are children of
              Kronos,
       they who fought from lofty Mount Othrys, the illustrious
              Titans,
       they who fought from Olympos, the gods who are givers of
              good things,
       whom the lovely-haired Rhea bore of her union with Kronos.
635 These had fought with each other for ten continuous years,
     striving in heart-rending battle and never relenting at all;
     and for this difficult strife there was no solution or end in
     either side's favor in sight; the balance of battle seemed equal.
     But when he had regaled them with the appropriate
              nourishment
640 of ambrosia and nectar, which are the foods of the gods,
     and the spirit of courage had grown in the breasts of them all
     from having eaten of nectar and of delicious ambrosia,
       then the Father of Gods and of Men addressed them as
              follows:
       "Listen to me, O glorious children of Gaia and Ouranos,
645 while I say what the heart in my breast is urging upon me.
     Now for a very long time we have fought for victory and
              mastery,
       coming against each other in battle day after day,

they the immortal Titans and we who are children of Kronos.
Come, I beg you, and show your mighty power to the Titans,
650 show your invincible hands against them in terrible warfare;
think of my kindness, my friendship to you, how after much
         suffering
you have returned to the light from torturous bondage below
         and
risen out of invisible darkness because I devised it."
Thus he spoke, and noble Kottos immediately answered him:
655 "What are you saying? We acknowledge your claim. We by
         experience
know for ourselves your superior mind, your superior sagacity.
You have become a shield for immortals from chilling disaster;
by your careful devising out of invisible darkness
we have returned, we have been freed from bondage secure,
660 we, unexpectedly blessed, are here, O Lord, Son of Kronos.
So now in purpose unbending, with spirits eager to help you
we shall grant your power our strength in terrible warfare,
fighting against the Titans in mighty encounters of battle."
Thus he spoke, and the gods, the givers of good things,
         applauded,
665 hearing his words; and now their spirits were eager for war
more than ever before. On that day they all together
stirred up horrible battle, both the males and the females,
they the immortal Titans and they who are children of
         Kronos and
those whom Zeus had brought to the light from below earth
         in Erebos,
670 who were frightening, mighty, of overpowering strength.
Each of them had one hundred arms which shot from his
         shoulders—
so many each of them had—and each of them had fifty heads
growing out of his shoulders over his powerful limbs.

COMMENT

We turn somewhat abruptly from the bondage of Prometheus at the end of the last passage to the bondage of the Hundred-Handers (a link is provided, as West points out, by the motif of bondage) and so back to the Succession Myth. On the advice of Gaia (a prophetic power) Zeus frees the Hundred-Handers after the gods and Titans have been fighting for ten long years.

That Zeus needs the Hundred-Handers in order to defeat the Titans seems to throw a shadow on his power. But perhaps their role is owing to an epic motif according to which, in a long, evenly fought battle, one side finally wins by taking the advice of an oracle and bringing in aid from the outside. We can compare the story of how the gods finally defeated the giants by bringing in the aid of Herakles on the advice of an oracle; compare Apollodoros Bibliotheka *1.6.1. Hesiod mitigates the fact of Zeus's dependency on the Hundred-Handers by emphasizing that they owe their freedom to his superior wisdom.*

Line 668 is a repetition of lines 631 and 648: "they the immortal Titans and they (we) who are children of Kronos." But the earlier occurrences are used to describe the fighting as equally balanced, whereas here the Hundred-Handers are added (669), thus tipping the balance in favor of the gods.

The battlefield is the plain of Thessaly, at the north of which is Mount Olympos from which the gods fight, and at the south of which is Mount Othrys from which the Titans fight. On a clear day Mount Olympos is visible from Mount Othrys about seventy miles away.

THE WAR WITH THE TITANS

The Final Battle

These then stood there facing the Titans in terrible warfare,

675 each with an enormous rock in each of his strong hands;

and the Titans on their side mustered their army's strength,

eager for battle. Both sides now were showing their force,
what their hands could accomplish. The boundless sea
    terribly echoed,
earth roared loudly, broad heaven above was shaken and
    groaned, and
680 high Olympos was trembling, for it was struck to its base
under the rushing immortals; the quaking caused by their feet
reached into shadowy Tartaros, as did the piercing noise
of their enormous onrush and the whir of their powerful
    missiles.
Thus they hurled against each other their pain-dealing
    missiles,
685 and the voices of both sides mounted to star-studded heaven,
as they attacked each other and clashed with enormous
    shouting.
Zeus no longer restrained his strength, but immediately now
    his
breast was filled with the spirit of might; now he was showing
all of his force; down from heaven and Olympos he came,
690 striding, rapidly hurling continuous lightning; his bolts were
closely flying one after the other out of his strong hand,
thunderous and flaming, causing an awesome fire to arise as
thickly they fell. The life-giving earth was everywhere crying,
burning with fire; vast forests were howling aloud;
695 earth was everywhere boiling, as were the streams of Okeanos
and the exhaustless sea. The hot blast beset the chthonian
Titans below, the immense fire reaching into darkness divine,
and the brilliantly shining glare produced by the flashing
bolt and the lightning blinded their eyes in spite of their
    might,
700 and an amazing heat possessed Chaos. If one had actually
seen this event or actually heard it, it would have seemed just
like what one would expect should the earth and the broad

sky above come

crashing together, for such a great deafening noise would
        arise if

earth were fallen upon by sky from on high falling down;

705 such was the noise that arose from this clash of immortals in
        combat.

Blasts of winds, roaring loudly, shook everything, stirred up
        the dust,

carried forward the thunder and lightning and smoldering
        firebolt,

great Zeus's weapons; and they carried the shouting and
        shrieking

into the center of conflict; a frightening clamor arose as

710 the armies horribly clashed and showed their works of war.

Now the balance of battle inclined. Before this they had

ceaselessly fought with each other in mighty encounters of
        battle.

Now in the forefront Kottos, Briareos, and Gyges stood,

rousing wild-spirited warfare, beings who thirsted for battle,

715 who were sending again and again from their powerful hands

three hundred rocks; and so with these missiles they covered
        the Titans

and then ushered them down into the wide-wayed earth,

where they bound them securely in bondage grievous to bear,

having by force of their hands defeated them though they
        were mighty.

720 Under the earth they put them as far as the sky is above earth,

for so far is shadowy Tartaros under the earth.

COMMENT

*Zeus with his thunderbolts and the Hundred-Handers with their
rocks are the only fighters described. We are first told of the fighting
of Zeus, his* aristeia. *An* aristeia *is the great heroic action of a*

fighter, like that of Diomedes in the fifth book of the Iliad. *Among its characteristic features are the inspiration of the hero to fight at full strength, his arming, and his rushing into battle against the enemy. Thus Zeus, when he has gathered his full strength, rushes from Mount Olympos armed with his thunderbolts. As West notes, his fiery attack is like that of the Lord in Psalm 97:3–4:*

> *Fire goes before him*
> *and burns up his enemies all around.*
> *The world is lit up beneath his lightning-flash;*
> *the earth sees it and writhes in pain.*

Although the fighting of the Hundred-Handers is described after that of Zeus, it is really contemporaneous with it. At the end of the description of Zeus's fighting we are told that his thunderbolts blind the Titans in the Underworld; and it is here, in Tartaros, that the Hundred-Handers are finally said to imprison them.

THE DESCRIPTION OF THE UNDERWORLD

If an anvil of bronze should fall from the sky, it would travel
nine days and nights before on the tenth day coming to earth;
and if an anvil of bronze should fall from the earth, it would
    travel
725 nine days and nights before on the tenth day coming to
      Tartaros.
A wall of bronze has been built around Tartaros, and over
      this wall,
surrounding its neck, Night is poured in three layers, above
      which
rise the roots of the earth and the springs of the exhaustless
      sea.
There, in Tartaros, the immortal Titans are hidden under
730 darkness invisible, as Zeus of the Storm Cloud wills them
      to be,

down in that place of decay at huge earth's outermost limits.
To them is left no escape, for Poseidon has set there a bronze
     door,
and at the sides of this door the wall, encircling them, meets;
and here Gyges, Kottos, and mighty-hearted Briareos
735 have their abodes, guards ever faithful to Zeus of the Aigis.
There for the dusky earth and for shadowy Tartaros
and for the exhaustless sea and for star-studded sky,
for all things, the sources and ends are set in due order,
the terrible and moldering ends, hateful even to gods,
740 in an enormous chasm: not even after falling a full year
would one arrive at its bottom once he had got through its
     gates,
but here and there would be carried by gust upon gust of
     terribly
blowing wind; and this is a frightening portent even for
gods immortal. And there stands black Night's frightening
     house,
745 being deeply hidden from view, covered with dark clouds.
Before this stands the son of Iapetos holding the broad sky,
using his head and weariless arms for steady support,
where Night exchanges greetings with Day when they are
     drawing
near to each other and crossing their great threshold of
     bronze.
750 One is returning home while the other is going abroad,
and they are never together at home at the same time:
one is always away from their house and out in the world
wandering the earth; the other is always staying at home and
waiting for her time to come to start on her journey again.
755 One of them, Day, brings far-seeing Light for men on the
     earth;
the other one, baneful Night, covered with dark clouds, holds

Hypnos (Sleep) in her hands, the brother of Thanatos (Death).
There, nearby, is the house where Hypnos and Thanatos
    dwell,
black Night's children, frightening gods, upon whom shining
760 Helios, the sun, never looks with his luminous rays,
either when ascending the sky or when descending it.
One of them, Hypnos, crossing the earth and the sea's broad
    expanse,
quietly makes his rounds and soothingly comes to men;
the other one, Thanatos, has a heart made of iron, a pitiless
765 heart of bronze in his breast, and he keeps every man he
seizes upon, and even to gods immortal is hateful.
There, farther on, stands the echoing house of the God of the
    Underworld,
and a frightening dog is on guard in front of its entrance,
770 one who is pitiless and knows a terrible trick: he welcomes
everyone entering by wagging his tail and putting his ears
    down,
but he allows no one to escape, but keeping a close watch
swallows whomever he catches emerging out of the gates.
775 And there abides that goddess who is hateful to the immortals,
frightening Styx, the oldest daughter of circling Okeanos.
She has a dwelling apart from the gods in a glorious palace,
which has a roof consisting of great rocks, and all around it,
on every side, are columns of silver reaching to heaven.
780 Rare are the times when the daughter of Thaumas, swift-
    footed Iris,
goes to and fro on her mission across the broad back of the sea,
when some strife or quarrel arises among the immortals
and one of those who dwell in Olympian homes speaks falsely;
then Zeus sends Iris to bring from afar in a pitcher of gold
785 some of that much-invoked water for use in the gods' great
    oath.

Cold is this water that comes pouring forth out of a towering,
very precipitious rock; far down under wide-wayed earth it
flows through the black night from Okeanos's sacred river,
for Styx has as her share a tenth of the streams of Okeanos.
790 Nine parts of Okeanos, which circles the earth and the sea's
broad expanse,
whirling with silvery eddies empty into the main;
but that part that flows from the rock brings gods a great
torment.
If a god who dwells on the peaks of snowy Olympos
perjures himself while pouring libation of water of Styx,
795 he must lie without any breath till a year is complete and
never go to enjoy the food of ambrosia and nectar,
but he must lie in his well-covered bed afflicted with sickness,
breathless and speechless, held in the grip of a terrible coma.
And when a great year has passed and this sickness has come
to an end,
800 still he has labors to do, increasingly difficult labors,
being without any share in the life of immortals for nine years,
never going to share in their councils or in their feasts for
nine full years. But then in the tenth year again he can share in
gatherings of the immortals who dwell in Olympian homes.
805 Such is the oath that the gods ordained by Styx's unfailing,
primeval water which flows through the rugged area below.
There for the dusky earth and for shadowy Tartaros
and for the exhaustless sea and for star-studded sky,
for all things, the sources and ends are set in due order,
810 the terrible and moldering ends, hateful even to gods.
There are the glittering gates and the threshold of bronze,
which is unshakable, a natural formation, since it is fixed with
deep-reaching roots. Farther down still and far from all gods,
over the darkness of Chaos, the Titans have their abodes.
815 And the glorious assistants of Zeus the Loud Thunderer also

dwell in a house down here at Okeanos's ultimate sources:
Kottos, Gyges, and Briareos; and roaring, earth-shaking
      Poseidon
because of Briareos's goodliness has made him his son-in-law,
giving him wave-riding Kymopoleia, his daughter, in
      marriage.

COMMENT

*The description of the Underworld is a geographical catalog that
deals with some of the same divinities we have seen in the preceding
genealogical catalogs: Night and Day, Hypnos and Thanatos, and
Styx. These divinities, as well as the God of the Underworld, are
concerned with the lives of gods and men above.*

   *We are first given the picture of the universe as a three-story
structure with heaven as its top, earth in its middle, and Tartaros
at its bottom. The space between Tartaros and earth is described as
the source of everything, and is called a chasm (740), which is
apparently another name for Chaos.*

   *Styx is given the longest description because of her importance
as the water by which the gods swear their great oath. False-
swearing gods are punished by being made completely helpless for
a year and then by having to suffer a nine-year period of labors
in exile from Olympos. The repeated mention of Olympos as the
home of the gods (783, 793, 804) is like the naming of a beloved
city to which it is a great privilege to belong. Perjury is a very
disrupting evil in any society. It is forbidden by one of the Ten
Commandments. We shall find that Hesiod is much concerned with
it in W.D.*

ZEUS DEFEATS HIS LAST ENEMY,
THE MONSTER TYPHOEUS

820 But when Zeus had driven the Titans from heaven in
      banishment,

Zeus fighting Typhoeus—from a painting on a vase of the sixth century B.C. in the Antikensammlungen, Munich. Zeus is wielding his thunderbolt. This depiction of Typhoeus is very different from Hesiod's description, the artist apparently feeling incapable of rendering a hundred serpentine heads; compare Theog. 820ff.

huge Gaia brought forth the last of her children, Typhoeus,
    having
mingled in love with Tartaros through Aphrodite the
    Golden.
Wonderfully strong were the arms of Typhoeus to do all he
    wanted;
he had the weariless feet of a mighty divinity; and out of his
825 shoulders a hundred heads of a serpent, a frightening dragon,
rose, each of which shot forth a flickering black tongue; and
    out of his
eyes flashed fire from under the brows of each of his heads,
fire came blazing forth from each of his staring heads;
and from each of his terrible heads he was able to speak and
830 utter every imaginable sound. Sometimes the sound was
speech, the language the gods understand, sometimes the
    bellowing
wail of a bull, a thunderous roll, an ominous rumble,
sometimes the roar of a lion with heart unrelenting and
    ruthless,
sometimes the whimpering squeal of a dog, a marvel to hear,
835 sometimes a hiss. The mountains around were ringing with
    echoes.
On that day an incurable disaster would have occurred and
now Typhoeus would rule as king of immortals and mortals,
if the Father of Gods and of Men had not been attentive.
Thunder came from him, pure thunder and mighty, and
    everywhere earth
840 horribly echoed in answer, as did the broad sky above and
Pontos, the sea, the streams of Okeanos, and Tartaros below.
Great Olympos was quivering under the feet of the god,
under the rush of the King; earth was groaning in answer.
Flames, emitted by both sides, enveloped the shadowy sea,

845   flames from the thunder and lightning and from the fire of
          the monster,
      flames from the withering fire-blasts and from the shattering
          firebolts.
      Earth was everywhere boiling, as were the sky and the sea.
      High waves were dashing on headland and shore, covering
          the earth,
      stirred by the force of those rushing immortals; the quaking
          was terrible.
850   Hades, the king of the dead and departed, was frightened
          below,
      as were the Titans in Tartaros, where they were gathered with
          Kronos,
      such a great ceaseless clamor arose of terrible warfare.
      So when Zeus had collected his strength and caught up his
          weapons,
      which are the roaring thunder and lightning and smoldering
          firebolt,
855   then did he, swooping down from Olympos, strike him and
          burn off
      all the marvelous heads of that very frightening monster.
      And he, being subdued with lashing blow upon blow,
      fell on his knees in defeat, and huge Gaia groaned in response.
      Fire spurted out of that god, that thunder-bolted divinity,
860   when he was struck in the glens of the mountain, the rocky
          Aidna,
      into submission. And huge Gaia, burning with fire
      under the marvelous blast, melted even as tin melts
      when in a well-pierced melting pot clever young blacksmiths
          skillfully
      heat it; or as hard iron, which is the strongest of metals,
865   being subdued in the glens of a mountain by blazing-hot fire,

melts in the divine earth under the hands of Hephaistos.
So in the light of that bright conflagration Gaia was melting.
And in his anger Zeus hurled him into the vastness of
    Tartaros.
Out of Typhoeus arises the strength of wet-blowing winds,
870 which we distinguish from Boreas, Notos, and sky-clearing
    Zephyros,
winds that belong to the race of the gods and benefit mortals.
These others are winds which recklessly play on the face of
    the deep,
these the winds which fall from above on the shadowy sea and
cause great havoc for mortals, rushing in terrible blasts;
875 this way now, now that way they blow, scattering ships and
bringing sailors to ruin; no way is left of escape for
men caught out on the sea whenever such stormwinds attack.
These are the winds which blow on the vast earth's flowering
    fields and
ruin the beautiful crops of earth-engendered men,
880 everywhere piling up dust and raising a terrible roar.

COMMENT

It is somewhat surprising to find Gaia producing an enemy of Zeus, but this is probably to be explained by the fact that monsters like Typhoeus are naturally thought of as arising out of the earth.

The aristeia *of Zeus against Typhoeus should be compared with his* aristeia *against the Titans. Aidna, the place of Typhoeus's defeat, was in later antiquity identified with Mount Aitna (Etna) in Sicily, but it seems likely that Hesiod located it somewhere in Asia Minor. Zeus hurls Typhoeus into Tartaros, and destructive winds are said to arise from him there. This is an aetiological myth used to explain the fierceness of such winds. We should note that our word typhoon, though influenced by Typhon (an alternate form of Typhoeus), is derived from the Chinese for "great wind."*

It is certain that Typhoeus originated in the Near East. As pointed

out in the Introduction, he plays the same role in Greek mythology
as Tiamat in Babylonian mythology, Ullikummi in Hittite-Hur-
rian mythology, and Yamm or Lotan in Phoenician mythology.
Typhoeus's most prominent feature is his hundred serpentine heads.
We can compare the description of the many-headed Leviathan,
another product of Near Eastern mythology, in Psalm 74:12–14:

> *But thou, O God, thou king from of old,*
> *thou mighty conqueror all the world over,*
> *by thy power thou didst cleave the sea monster in two*
> *and break the sea serpent's heads above the waters;*
> *thou didst crush Leviathan's many heads*
> *and throw him to the people of the wilderness for food.*

THE KINGSHIP OF ZEUS AND HIS MARRIAGES

But when the blessed gods had finished the struggle of
      fighting,
when they had won in the war with the Titans the contest
      for honors,
then they, following the advice of Gaia, urged the Olympian
far-seeing Zeus to rule as their lord and take up the kingship
885 over immortals; and so he fairly apportioned their honors.
Zeus the King of the Gods took as his first wife Metis,
who among gods and mortal men was the wisest of all.
But when her time came to bear him the gray-eyed goddess
      Athena,
then he, deceiving her mind by means of a trick and using
890 flattering words to beguile her, put her into his stomach,
following the advice of Gaia and of star-studded Ouranos.
So they advised him in order that no one besides Zeus, no
      other
one of the ever-living gods, might possess the honor of
      kingship.

Metis, they said, was going to bear him two powerful
    children:
895 first a daughter, the gray-eyed goddess Tritogeneia,
who would equal her father in strength and excellent counsel;
then a son who would be the King of Gods and of Men;
she was going to bear him a son of invincible might.
But before this could happen Zeus put her into his stomach
900 so that this goddess might help him to plan both good things
    and bad.
    Then he took as his wife shining Themis, who bore him the
        Horai:
    Orderly Government, Justice, and Peace, a bountiful
        goddess;
    and the Moirai, whom Zeus of the Counsels gave greatest
        honor:
905 Klotho, Lachesis, Atropos, powers that determine the fates
    and
grant to mortal men to have both good things and bad.
Then Eurynome, the daughter of Okeanos, a beautiful girl,
bore of her union with him the three lovely-cheeked Graces:
bright Aglaia, joyful Euphrosyne, charming Thalia.
910 Love which drops from their eyes strikes whomever they
    look on,
    loosening his limbs; under their brows their eyes glance with
        loveliness.
    Next he came to the bed of Demeter, the feeder of many,
    and she bore him white-armed Persephone, who was by
        Hades
    seized from her dear mother's side, as Zeus of the Counsels
        permitted.
915 Then he mingled in love with the lovely-haired Mnemosyne,
and she bore him the Muses crowned with headbands of gold,

nine of them, who are delighters in feasts and the joy of the
song.
Then Leto bore him Apollo and Artemis, expert in archery,
children surpassing in beauty all other descendants of
Ouranos;

920 these she conceived by mingling in love with Zeus of the
Aigis.
Last of all it was Hera he took as his blossoming bride,
and she bore him Hebe and Ares and Eileithyia
when she had mingled in love with the King of Gods and of
Men.
Then he produced of himself from his head the gray-eyed
Athena,

925 frightening rouser and leader of armies, the weariless one,
who is the mistress delighting in war and the tumult of battle.
And Hera, angered with him and trying to rival her husband,
bore of herself without mingling in love glorious Hephaistos,
who surpasses in skill of his hands all descendants of Ouranos.

COMMENT

*Now Zeus is acclaimed King of the Gods and apportions their
honors to the various divinities. We remember his promise to Styx
and the other earlier powers to honor them properly if they helped
him in the war with the Titans. The division of honors is like the
division of booty after a war.*

*Zeus's wives and children are important powers in his new gov-
ernment of the world. This is especially evident in his marriages
with Metis and Themis, his first two wives. By Metis (Wisdom)
he is destined to have, in addition to Athena, a son who will drive
him from the kingship; but he thwarts this fate by swallowing her.
Perhaps, as West suggests, he tricks her by persuading her to revert
to her natural element, water, for she is an Okeanid. Thus the
Succession Myth is brought to an end; there will be no son to
overthrow Zeus, as there was for Ouranos and Kronos. Moreover,*

by swallowing Metis (Wisdom), Zeus is able to plan good and bad things, and to sire the Moirai who give good and bad things to men. Line 906 echoes line 900.

Themis (Law) bears him the Horai (the Hours or Seasons, who are spirits of limits) and the Moirai (the Fates). The Horai are Orderly Government, Justice, and Peace, closely associated powers and of much importance to Hesiod in W.D. *The Moirai are here called Klotho (Spinster), Lachesis (Dispenser of Lots), and Atropos (Inflexible), and are said to give men good things (such as life, health, and wealth) and bad things (such as disease, old age, and death). We have already seen them listed (without individual names) as the children of Night and avengers of wrongdoing in* Theog. *217ff. See the Comment on this passage for possible explanations of their double parentage.*

Scholars disagree about where the original Theog. *ends. An early stop, at line 900, is suggested by West. I am inclined to agree with other scholars, like Marg, who would take it through line 929. Since the Metis passage looks forward to the birth of Athena, the description of Athena's birth makes a good concluding ring-composition, and the contrast between Hephaistos and Athena strikes a very Hesiodic note. These divinities represent two different kinds of strife, that of war and that of peaceful competition. We can compare the contrast between the two kinds of Eris (Strife) in* W.D. *11ff.*

MORE UNIONS OF ZEUS AND OTHER GODS AND GODDESSES

930 And Amphitrite bore to the roaring Shaker of Earth
Triton, a mighty, wide-ruling power, who with his mother
and with his lordly father holds the depths of the sea and
dwells in a gold house, a frightening god. And Aphrodite,
queen of Kythera, to shield-piercing Ares bore Phobos and
          Deimos,
935 frightening powers who accompany Ares the Sacker of Cities

as they scatter the thick ranks of men in the onslaught of
  chill war;
and she bore Harmonia, the wife of high-spirited Kadmos.
And Maia, the daughter of Atlas, bore the herald of the gods,
glorious Hermes, to Zeus, after mounting his sacred bed.
940 And Semele, the daughter of Kadmos, having mingled in love
  with Zeus,
bore him a shining son, Dionysos the Bringer of Joy,
she a mortal producing a god; now both are immortals.
And Alkmene gave birth to the wonderful strength of
  Herakles,
when she and Zeus of the Storm Cloud had mingled together
  in love.
945 And Hephaistos, the far-famed god who is lame in both legs,
took Aglaia, the youngest Grace, as his blossoming bride.
And golden-haired Dionysos took the blond Ariadne,
who was the daughter of Minos, as his blossoming bride;
and she was made an unaging immortal by Zeus, son of
  Kronos.
950 And powerful Herakles, the valiant son of fair-ankled
  Alkmene,
when he had finished his strenuous labors, married Hebe,
who was the daughter of almighty Zeus and golden-shod
  Hera;
she became his praiseworthy wife on snowy Olympos,
where, his great work complete, among the immortals he
  blessedly
955 dwells, living the life of a painless, unaging divinity.
And Perseis, one of Okeanos's glorious daughters,
to weariless Helios bore Kirke and King Aietes.
And Aietes, the son of Helios the Bringer of Light,
married by will of the gods Idyia, a lovely-cheeked girl,

960 a daughter of Okeanos, the river that flows in unending
         completion;
  and she bore him fair-ankled Medeia, when she had come and
  yielded to him in love through Aphrodite the Golden.
  Farewell now, you gods who have your homes on Olympos,
  and you islands and mainlands and salty sea lying within.

965 Now, O sweet-sounding voices, Muses who dwell on
         Olympos,
  daughters of Zeus of the Aigis, sing of the race of goddesses,
  of all those who lay in love with mortal men and
  bore, they being immortal, children resembling the gods.
  Demeter gave birth to Ploutos, she a goddess divine

970 having mingled in passionate love with the hero Iasion,
  lying with him in a thrice-plowed field of Krete's fertile island;
  goodly Ploutos goes over earth and the sea's broad back
  everywhere, granting the good luck of wealth and a blessed
         existence
  to all whomever he meets and into whose hands he comes.

975 And Harmonia, the daughter of golden Aphrodite,
  bore to Kadmos in the well-crowned city of Thebes
  Ino, Semele, lovely-cheeked Agaue, Autonoe,
  who was the wife of the long-haired Aristaios, and Polydoros.
  And Kallirhoe, who was one of Okeanos's daughters,

980 when she had mingled in love with mighty-hearted Chrysaor
  through Aphrodite the Golden, bore him the strongest of all
         men,
  Geryon, whom the wonderful power of Herakles slew
  as he defended his shambling herd in the isle Erytheia.
  And Eos bore to Tithonos bronze-helmeted Memnon,

985 the Ethiopians' king, and the lordly Emathion.
  And she bore of Kephalos's love a glorious son,
  powerful Phaethon, who was a man resembling the gods.

On his coming of age, in the tender flower of young manhood,
while still boyish in thought, smile-loving Aphrodite,
990 seizing and carrying him off, made him a spirit divine
dwelling within her holy temple's innermost shrine.
And Medeia, the daughter of Zeus-nurtured King Aietes,
Aison's son, Iason, by will of the immortal gods
took as his wife, when he had finished his strenuous labors,
995 those many tasks which Pelias, that great, overbearing king,
that hybristic, wicked worker of outrage, had ordered.
When with a great deal of trouble he had completed these
      labors,
Aison's son in his swift ship sailed back home to Iolkos
with that girl of the bright eyes and made her his blossoming
      bride.
1000 And Medeia in love with Iason, a shepherd of people,
bore him a son, Medeios, whom Philyra's offspring Cheiron
reared in the mountains; so great Zeus's purpose was
      brought to fulfillment.
And one of the daughters of Nereus, the Old Man of the Sea,
the divine goddess Psamathe, gave birth to Phokos,
1005 when she had mingled with Aiakos through Aphrodite the
      Golden;
and another, the goddess silver-foot Thetis, having
yielded to Peleus's love, bore man-slaying, lion-hearted
      Achilleus.
And Aphrodite, the lovely-crowned goddess of Kythera,
bore Aineias, when she had lain in passionate love with
1010 the hero Anchises in the heights of the many-valed, windy
      Mount Ida.
And Kirke, the daughter of Helios, the son of Hyperion,
bore, after mingling in love with much-enduring Odysseus,
blameless Agrios and the mighty hero Latinos.

1015 These in a region remote, in islands secluded and holy,
     rule over all the Tyrsenians, a people of great renown.
     And the divine goddess Kalypso bore to Odysseus,
     when they had mingled in love, Nausithoos and Nausinoos.
     These, then, are those goddesses who lay in love with mortal
         men and
1020 bore, they being immortal, children resembling the gods.
     Now, O sweet-sounding voices, Muses who dwell on
         Olympos,
     daughters of Zeus of the Aigis, sing of the race of women.

COMMENT

*This final section consists of two catalogs. The first (930–64) is
a miscellaneous list including three unions of Zeus resulting in the
births of Hermes, Dionysos, and Herakles.*

*The second (965–1020) is a catalog of goddesses. It seems unlikely
that Hesiod composed the entry on Kallirhoe, the mother of Geryon
by Chrysaor, since the same information has already been given in
lines 287ff. We should note that the Mount Ida on which Aphro-
dite has her affair with Anchises is in the region of Troy and not
on Krete. Their son, Aineias (Aeneas), according to later tradition,
fled to Italy after the Trojan War and became the father of the
Roman people. Agrios and Latinos, the sons of Kirke (Circe) by
Odysseus, are said to rule over the Tyrsenians, that is, the Tyrr-
henians, another name of the Etruscans. Agrios ("The Wild One")
is perhaps to be identified with the Latin Faunus, who is some-
times described by the adjective* agrestis, *"wild"; and Latinos is
the eponymous hero of the Latin people.*

The last two lines (1021–22) introduce the Catalog of Women.
*This was a long poem, known to us now only in fragments. It is
doubtful whether Hesiod composed it.*

Works and Days

AN INTRODUCTORY HYMN TO ZEUS

Pierian Muses, I pray you, singers and bringers of glory,
come and tell us of Zeus, singing a hymn of your father,
through whom mortal men are both dishonored and honored;
they become famous and do not become famous as almighty
       Zeus wills.

5 Easily he strengthens the faltering, easily shatters the strong,
easily makes the flourishing fade, the faded to flourish,
easily straightens the crooked and withers the haughty in
       spirit,
Zeus the Thunderer on High, who dwells in the uppermost
       palace.
Hearken, O witnessing, listening Zeus, and straighten our
       judgments,

10 hold us to justice. I for my part would tell Perses the truth.

COMMENT

*The Pierian Muses are invoked, Pieria being the place of their birth
near the home of their father on the top of Mount Olympos. Then
we are given a short hymn to Zeus that is comparable to the long
hymn to the Muses at the beginning of* Theog. *Zeus is praised
for his ability to do exactly opposite things. We can compare the
description of God in 1 Samuel 2:6–7:*

93

> *The Lord killeth, and maketh alive;*
> *He bringeth down to the grave, and bringeth up.*
> *The Lord maketh poor, and maketh rich;*
> *He bringeth low, He also lifteth up.*

Moreover, Zeus is a witnessing and listening god who maintains justice among men. No evildoer is able to escape the attention and so the punishment of the god who sees and hears everything (compare R. Pettazzoni, The All-Knowing God, *tr. H. J. Rose* [London, 1956]*).*

Hesiod concludes his hymn to Zeus by announcing his intention to speak the truth to his brother Perses in W.D. *We are reminded of how the Muses in* Theog. *28 inspire him to speak the truth. In the following section he shows his concern for truth by amplifying a statement in* Theog.

THE TWO KINDS OF ERIS

No, there is not just one kind of Eris present upon earth,
but there are two. The man who is wise would give praise to
    the one,
blame to the other; their spirits are so completely opposed.
One of them, she of the hard heart, stirs up the evil of war and
15 conflict of battle, and no mortal loves her, but under
    compulsion,
as the immortals decree, we honor the burdensome Eris.
But the other, who is the older daughter of black Night,
Zeus, son of Kronos, ruling on high and dwelling in
    brightness,
put in the roots of the earth, and she is much better for men.
20 She sets a man to his work in spite of the fact that he's shiftless,
for it makes him eager to work whenever he sees
another prospering, one who is hastening to plow and plant
    and

EPIS

The bad Eris (Strife)—from a painting on a vase of the archaic period; Berlin, no. F 1775. Compare W.D. *11ff.*

build an excellent homestead. Neighbor is envious of
    neighbor

hastening to wealth, and this is the Eris that benefits mortals.

25 Potter fiercely challenges potter, carpenter carpenter,
beggar enviously strives with beggar, singer with singer.
Perses, I beg you to see that you cherish this truth in your
    heart and

let not the Eris who revels in evil keep you from work
listening to legal disputes, a spectator idling in public.

30 Little concern for legal disputes and cases at law has
he for whom there is not a sufficiency stored within of
seasonably gathered grain, earth's produce, the fruit of
        Demeter.

This got in plenty, then you might stir up cases and conflicts
over others' possessions. But you'll not have a second chance

35 now to be doing so. Let us immediately settle our differences,
using straight verdicts of justice, those that are Zeus-sent and
    best.

Past is the time when we went into court to divide our
    inheritance

and you departed with more than your fair share by indulging
    the kings,

gift-eating men, who are willing to exercise this sort of justice.

40 Fools, they don't know how much more the half is than the
    whole

nor how much nourishment there is in mallow and asphodel.

COMMENT

The bad Eris (Strife) is listed in Theog. *225ff. among the children
of Night. She is the mother of powers of war and also of legal
dispute, among whom is the oath-god Horkos who punishes perjury.
Here Hesiod adds her sister, the good Eris, who drives men to
compete with each other and so to earn an honest living. The two*

kinds of Eris can be thought of as the two main motivating forces of W.D., comparable to Eros as the main motivating force of Theog. The bad Eris stirs up legal disputes and raises the demand for justice, while the good Eris sets men to work. Perses is exhorted to work and warned against doing injustice, as he had done in his case with Hesiod over their inheritance by bribing the nobles (called "kings" in the text) who acted as judges.

These nobles are described as gift-eaters (that is, takers of bribes in the form of food), and are said not to understand two proverbs that apparently mean the same thing: half a loaf with justice is better than a whole loaf with injustice. Mallow and the root of the asphodel were poor men's food. We can compare Psalm 37:16: "Better is the little which the righteous has than the great wealth of the wicked." The presupposition of Hesiod's proverbs is that man must work for his living, and that this is so because the gods have willed it.

THE PROMETHEUS-PANDORA STORY

For the gods keep hidden the livelihood of men.
Otherwise you might easily do enough work in a day to
have enough for a full year with no further need to be
    working,
45 and might immediately hang up your rudder in the smoke of
    your fireplace
and release your oxen and hardworking mules from their
    labor.
But Zeus hid our livelihood when he was angered at heart
because Prometheus, the clever deviser, tried to deceive him.
This is why he devised anguishing miseries for men.
50 And he hid fire, which the goodly son of Iapetos stole back,
taking it from Zeus of the Counsels to give it to men, secretly
carrying it in a fennel stalk's hollow from Zeus of the Firebolt.

Then, stirred to anger, Zeus of the Storm Cloud addressed
       him as follows:
"Son of Iapetos, you who surpass all others in planning,
55 you rejoice in your theft of my fire and in having deceived me,
      being the cause of great pain to yourself and men in the
          future.
I shall give them in payment of fire an evil which all shall
take to their hearts with delight, an evil to love and embrace."
Thus the Father of Gods and of Men addressed him, and
      laughed.
60 And he commanded far-famed Hephaistos immediately to
      make it
out of water and clay, and give it the voice of a human and
put in it strength and cause it to look like a goddess immortal,
having the lovely, desirable shape of a virgin. And then he
ordered Athena to teach her the skill of intricate weaving.
65 And Aphrodite the Golden he ordered to shed on her charm
      and
make her an object of painful love and exhausting desire.
And he ordered Hermes the Guide, the Slayer of Argos,
to put in her mind a dog's shamelessness and the deceit of a
      thief.
Thus spoke their king, Zeus, son of Kronos, and they obeyed
      him.
70 Immediately the famous Lame-Legged One molded of clay
an image resembling a virgin demure, as Zeus had decreed.
And the goddess gray-eyed Athena girdled and dressed her:
the Graces divine along with our Lady Persuasion hung
golden necklaces on her, and the lovely-haired Horai
75 crowned her head by setting upon it a garland of spring
      flowers,

all of which things Pallas Athena arranged in good order.
And the Guide, the Slayer of Argos, enclosed in her breast
lies and wheedling words and the treacherous ways of a thief,
following Zeus the Thunderer's decree; and he, heaven's
    herald,
80 gave her a speaking voice and announced that her name was
    Pandora,
"The Gift of All," because all the gods who dwell on Olympos
gave a gift to this plague for men who are eaters of bread.
But when he had completed this sheer inescapable snare,
Zeus Father had her led off as a gift to Epimetheus
85 by the famous Slayer of Argos, heaven's swift herald.
And Epimetheus took no heed of Prometheus's advice
not to receive any gift the Olympian Zeus might send him
but to reject it lest some evil should happen to mortals.
So he received it and learned by experience the evil he had.
90 For the tribes of men had previously lived on the earth
free and apart from evils, free from burdensome labor
and from painful diseases, the bringers of death to men.
In the power of these evils men rapidly pass into old age.
But then woman, raising the jar's great lid in her hands and
95 scattering its contents, devised anguishing miseries for men.
Only Hope was left within, securely imprisoned,
caught there under the lip of the jar, unable to fly
out and away, for before this could happen she let the lid
    drop,
as the Lord of the Aigis, Zeus of the Storm Cloud, decreed.
100 But as for those others, those numberless miseries, they
    wander among men,
for the earth is abounding in evils and so is the sea.
And diseases come upon men by day and by night,

everywhere moving at will, bringing evil to mortals
silently, for Zeus of the Counsels has deprived them of voices.
105 Thus in no way can anyone escape the purpose of Zeus.

COMMENT

*The Prometheus-Pandora story, which is the first of two comple-
mentary myths on the human condition, is primarily aimed at ex-
plaining why men must work for their livelihood. Pandora, the
first woman, is sent as a punishment to men in payment of Pro-
metheus's stealing fire for them, and she alters the former state of
blessedness by releasing the evils of our present condition from a
great jar (a pithos, which was used to store grain; West points out
that its identification as a pyxis, or box, is probably owing to a
lapse by Erasmus). Personified diseases come out of the jar; they
move about freely and silently, like invisible bacteria. One of them
is no doubt hunger, or malnutrition, which man must try to avoid
by working.*

*Only Hope, which man still controls, is left in the jar. Hope
seems to be a good in that it spurs men to action and consoles them
in misfortune; but in* W.D. *498ff., Hesiod speaks of a bad kind of
hope in which the shiftless poor man foolishly indulges when he
ought to be working. Hope is a poor substitute for the complete
foreknowledge possessed by Zeus, who lacks the need to hope since
he can bring his will to fulfillment.*

*The creation of the first woman is described at greater length
here than in the comparable passage in* Theog. *570ff. More gods
are involved, probably in anticipation of the announcement of her
significant name, Pandora, "The Gift of All." In* Theog., *as befits
a genealogical poem, man's fate is described in terms of the bachelor's
dilemma about whether or not to marry, while here it is described
in terms of the opening of a great storage jar, as better befits a poem
on farming.*

THE STORY OF THE AGES OF MAN

Now if you please I shall sketch another story for you,
telling it well and skillfully, and beg you deeply to ponder
how the gods and mortal men are born from the same source.
First of all the immortals who dwell in Olympian homes
110 brought into being the golden race of mortal men.
These belonged to the time when Kronos ruled over heaven,
and they lived like gods without any care in their hearts,
free and apart from labor and misery. Nor was the terror of
old age upon them, but always with youthful hands and feet
        they
115 took their delight in festive pleasures apart from all evil;
and they died as if going to sleep. Every good thing was
theirs to enjoy: the grain-giving earth produced her fruits
spontaneously, abundantly, freely; and they in complete
        satisfaction
lived off their fields without any cares in blessed abundance.
120 They were rich in flocks and dear to the blessed gods.
But when this race had been hidden under the cover of earth,
they became, as almighty Zeus decreed, divinities,
powers of good on the earth, guardians of mortal men,
who keep a watch on cases at law and hard-hearted deeds,
125 being hidden in air and going all over the earth,
blessing men with wealth, as this is their kingly right.
Then, after these, the gods who dwell in Olympian homes
created the second, the silver race, much worse than the first,
being unlike the golden both in thought and appearance.
130 Then the child spent a hundred years being nursed at home
under his mother's protecting care, playing, a great fool;
but when they had come to adulthood and man's full estate,
they had only a short time to live, and this with much torment

because of their folly, for they committed acts of ruinous
135 hybris against one another and refused to worship the gods
          and
offer the blessed ones sacrifice on their holy altars,
as is prescribed for men in their customs. So then these were
put out of sight by Zeus, son of Kronos, for he was angry
at their refusal to honor the blessed gods of Olympos.
140 But when this race had also been hidden under the earth,
they were called underground spirits, blessed mortal men,
who though second in rank still are given some honor.
Then Zeus Father created a third race of mortal men,
that which was bronze, one completely unlike the silver,
145 men sprung from ash trees, terrible and mighty, devoted to
          doing
war's wretched works and acts of hybris; nor did they eat any
bread but had in their bosoms strong-hearted spirits of
          adamant.
These were misshapen beings of great strength with
          invincible arms
growing out of their shoulders over their powerful limbs.
150 Bronze was the metal their weapons were made of, bronze
          were their houses,
bronze were the tools they used; the black metal iron came
          later.
These fell as victims to each other's slaughtering hands and
          went down
under the ground and into cold Hades' house of decay,
leaving no glory or name; in spite of their fearsomeness
155 black Death seized them and forced them to leave the bright
          light of the sun.
But when this race had also been hidden under the earth,
Zeus, son of Kronos, created another, a fourth race of men to

live on the boundless earth, one much juster and better,
which was the divine race of heroes. They are called
  demigods,
160 and are the race that lived earlier on the boundless earth.
These were destroyed by the evil of war and terrible battle,
some under seven-gated Thebes in the country of Kadmos,
  there brought
down to destruction when they were fighting for Oidipous's
  flocks;
others died after sailing across the great gulf of the sea to
165 Troy in order to fight for the right to the lovely-haired Helen.
There, to be sure, some met with the covering darkness of
  death;
but on others Zeus, son of Kronos, bestowed the blessing of
life and abodes far off from men at the ends of the earth.
170 There these dwell and take their delight with carefree hearts
off in the Isles of the Blessed by the streams of deep-swirling
  Okeanos,
fortunate heroes, for whom the grain-giving earth produces
a honey-sweet harvest three times a year, a bountiful yield.
Would that I now were no longer alive in the fifth age of men,
175 but had died earlier or had been born at a later time.
For we live in the age of the iron race, when men shall never
cease from labor and woe by day, and never be free from
anguish at night, for hard are the cares that the gods will
  be giving.
Yet there shall be even for these some good with the evil.
180 But Zeus shall also destroy this race of mortal men,
when their babies are born with their temples covered with
  gray hair.
Then the father will quarrel with his sons, the sons with their
  father,

guest will quarrel with host, comrade will quarrel with
     comrade,
nor will one's own brother be dear as in earlier times.
185 Men will dishonor their parents as soon as they see they are
     old,
finding them worthy of blame and cruelly railling against
     them,
hard-hearted children without any thought of divine
     retribution,
not repaying their parents grown old the price of their
     rearing.
Might will be justice; and one will destroy the other's city.
190 Neither will he who swears truly be favored nor he who is
     just nor
he who is good, but he will be granted promotion to honor
who is a doer of evil and hybris. Might will be justice and
shame will no longer exist. The bad will injure the good,
speaking crooked untruths and bearing false witness thereto.
195 Envy will be in attendance upon men, every miserable
     mortal,
causing commotion, rejoicing in evil, with face full of hate.
Then to Olympos retiring, leaving the broad-wayed earth,
wrapping their lovely forms in robes of gleaming white,
Shame and Nemesis, abandoning men, will return to their
     lives
200 among the immortals; and what will be left for mortal men are
only the anguishing pains, but no defense against evil.

COMMENT

*Hesiod introduces this story by asking Perses to keep in mind the
common origin of gods and men. He is probably alluding to the belief
that Earth was the original parent of both, and that men in the*

earliest times lived blessedly like gods. Such a state of blessedness was experienced by the golden race, but thereafter life degenerated as injustice, impiety, and hybris increased. The silver race is represented as a degeneration of the golden, the bronze of the silver, and the iron seems destined to be as bad as the bronze. The heroes are unique in that they show a break in this decline and are the only race not named after a metal. They had to be included because the Greeks thought of their ancestors as belonging to this heroic age (the period of Greek mythology), the two most important events of which were the Theban and Trojan wars.

Two different ideas are apparently combined in the description of the golden race: that of a golden age and that of an earlier blessed life under Kronos. The first is part of a myth of metallic ages, which, as West points out, may have originated in the Near East. It may belong to the same tradition as the description of the colossal statue in Daniel 2:31ff. (written much later than Hesiod). This statue is composed of five different substances—gold, silver, brass, iron, and iron mixed with clay—representing five successive kingdoms. The idea of a blessed life under Kronos, however, looks like a Greek invention, for there was a harvest festival called the Kronia, in which Kronos was honored as the king of an earlier blessed time. This idea of him is of course in conflict with his role in the Succession Myth, which is of Near Eastern origin.

The iron race is the one to which Hesiod belongs. He envisions its last days as a time when there will be a complete breakdown of justice. Babies will be born with gray hair—a fitting punishment for men who dishonor their old parents. The description of the iron race reminds us of Theog. *223ff., where Nemesis (Righteous Indignation) and the bad Eris are listed among the children of Night.*

THE FABLE OF THE HAWK AND THE NIGHTINGALE

Now I shall tell a fable to the perceptive kings.

Thus spoke the hawk to the nightingale, the speckle-necked
   bird,

as he was carrying her gripped in his talons high in the clouds,
205 and she was piteously crying, for she was pierced by the grip
of his
bent talons; thus he spoke and strongly advised her:
"Foolish thing, why are you shrieking? Your captor is much
stronger than you.
There shall you go wherever I take you though you're a
singer,
and, as I wish, I shall eat you for dinner or let you go free.
210 Foolish the man who wishes to fight against those who are
stronger;
he loses the victory and suffers pain in addition to shame."
Thus spoke the swift-flying hawk, the long-winged bird.

COMMENT

*The popularity of the animal fable among the Greeks is shown by
the collection attributed to Aisop, who is dated to the sixth century
B.C. Hesiod's fable is the earliest Greek example.*

*The hawk preaches to the nightingale as a wise man to a fool.
We can be sure that Hesiod is being ironic, for the nightingale (the
singer) must stand for himself and the hawk for the Boiotian kings
to whom he is telling the fable. Moreover, the moral drawn by the
hawk, that might makes justice, is the doctrine that will bring the
iron race to a calamitous end, and Hesiod denounces it in the following
section.*

AN EXHORTATION TO JUSTICE

But you, Perses, hearken to Justice and don't honor Hybris.
Hybris is a bad thing for the poor man, for not even the rich
man
215 easily bears it but staggers under its burdensome weight and
meets with calamity. Better it is to go on the road in

Justice (Dike) defeating Injustice (Adikia)—from a painting on a vase of the late sixth century B.C. *in the Kunsthistorisches Museum, Vienna. Compare W.D. 217f., where Justice is said to defeat the extreme injustice of Hybris.*

the other direction to Justice. Justice wins over Hybris,
finally coming in victor. The fool by suffering learns this.
For the oath-god Horkos runs after crooked injustice,
220 and there's an uproar when Justice is dragged off, when she is
            seized by
gift-eating men who interpret the laws with crooked decisions.
Justice departs deploring the city, its people and ways,
being hidden in air and bringing evil to men
who would make her an exile and do not apportion her
            straightly.
225 But for those who give justice to stranger and native alike,
straight pronouncements of justice, and stray not at all from
            her path,
theirs is a flourishing city, a people who prosper and grow.
Peace, the nurse of the young, is over their land, and they are
never afflicted with anguishing war by far-seeing Zeus.
230 Never do famine and ruin accompany men of straight justice,
but they enjoy in bountiful feasts the fruits of their labors.
Earth produces her plenty for them. The trees in the
            mountains
bear for them nuts on their outsides, swarms of bees in their
            centers.
Thick and soft is the wool which heavily covers their sheep.
235 And their wives are bearers of children resembling their
            fathers.
They abound in continuous plenty and have no need to
travel in ships, for the grain-giving earth provides them with
            food.
But upon those who are lovers of hybris and hard-hearted
            deeds
far-seeing Zeus, son of Kronos, dispenses his punishing
            justice.

240 Often even a whole city pays for the wrong of one person
    who is a doer of evil and worker of ruinous folly.
    Zeus, son of Kronos, sends terrible suffering from heaven
            upon them,
    famine together with plague, and makes the people to perish.
    Nor do their women bear children, but they have withering
            homes,
245 as the Olympian Zeus devises. And sometimes he makes them
    pay by giving their broad army defeat or bringing their wall
            down,
    or he, Zeus, son of Kronos, destroys their ships on the sea.
    Kings, I beg you to take careful note of this punishing justice,
    for there are here nearby among men immortal spirits
250 who take note of all who with crooked injustice trample
    each other down, having no thought of divine retribution.
    There are thirty thousand spirits on the bountiful earth,
    immortal sentinels of Zeus, strict guardians of mortal men,
    who keep a watch on cases at law and hard-hearted deeds,
255 being hidden in air and going all over the earth.
    And there is also the virgin Justice, the daughter of Zeus,
    who is honored and held in respect by the gods of Olympos.
    When she is harmed by anyone scorning her, crookedly
            speaking,
    she immediately goes to her seat by Zeus, son of Kronos, her
            father,
260 and informs on the unjust judge, so that the people
    pay for the crimes of their kings who making baneful
            decisions
    twist what is right into wrong with crooked pronouncements
            of justice.
    Beware of these things, O Kings, and see that you straighten
            your verdicts,

eaters of gifts, and no longer think of crooked decisions.

265 He who devises harm for another is harming himself,
and from the plan that is harmful most harm comes to the
          planner.
The eye of Zeus that sees all things and observes all things
now, if only it so wills, sees this state of affairs, and
this sort of justice that our city harbors does not escape it.

270 Now neither would I myself be just in my dealings with men
          nor
hope that my son be, since it will be a bad thing to be just,
if the deviser of greater injustice will have greater justice.
But I hope Zeus of the Counsels will not yet bring this to pass.
Perses, I beg you carefully to ponder these things in your
          heart and

275 hearken to Justice and think not at all of insolent might.
For this law is allotted to men by Zeus, son of Kronos:
fish and beasts of the wild and birds that fly in the air
eat one another, since Justice has no dwelling among them;
but to men he gives Justice, which is the greatest of blessings.

280 If one is willing to speak what he sees to be justice, what he
knows is the right thing, far-seeing Zeus grants him a blessed
          life.
But if he witnesses falsely and willfully perjures himself,
being a liar, a harmer of Justice, incurably blind,
he is leaving his family a gloomier future existence.

285 He who swears truly creates for his family future prosperity.

COMMENT

*In the long run justice will prove to be more powerful than hybris
(insolent violence). Zeus will bless the city of justice (its citizens
will live like the men of the golden race) but he will curse the city
of hybris. No wrongdoing, especially no injustice of the nobles
(Hesiod's "kings") acting as judges, escapes his notice. Men are*

forbidden to follow the law of violence according to which the
animals (like the hawk) live.

AN EXHORTATION TO WORK

Perses, you great fool, I shall advise you and try to improve
    you.
One can get for oneself Failure in pressing abundance
easily: smooth and exceedingly short is the road to her
    dwelling.
But the immortal gods require us to sweat in order to
290 reach Success: long and steep is the road to Success;
and it is rough at first, but when you have come to the top
then you will find that the going is easy in spite of the hardness.
He is the best man of all who perceives everything by himself,
seeing which of his courses will turn out better at last;
295 and he also is good who obeys one speaking the good.
But he who neither perceives by himself nor hearing another
takes to heart the advice he receives is utterly worthless.
But you, remembering always to do as I advise you,
work, Perses, you whose descent is divine, in order that you
    may
300 not be befriended by Hunger but by the revered lovely-
    crowned
goddess Demeter, who will fill up your barn with her plenty.
Hunger is a completely fitting companion for shiftless men.
Gods and men are angry with anyone who without working
lives with his spirit disposed like that of the stingless drones,
305 those nonworking consumers of what the toiling honeybees
labor to store. And see that you do your work in due order
that you may have each thing in its season to fill up your
    barns.

Men by the doing of work are rich in flocks and successful,
and if you work you will be much dearer to the immortals
310 and to mortal men, for they very much hate the shiftless.
Working is not a reproach, but not working is a reproach.
If you will work, the nonworker soon will be envious of you,
seeing you prosper; fame and honor attend upon wealth.
But whatever your god-given lot it is better to work,
315 better to turn your ruin-prone mind from others' possessions
and to be working and making your living as I advise you.
Shame, a bad kind of shame, attends on the man who is needy.
Shame is able greatly to hurt and greatly to help men.
Shame accompanies poverty; boldness comes with prosperity.

COMMENT

*We begin with a contrast between the road to Success and the road
to Failure. The Greek word translated as Success is* Arete *(more
literally Goodness); it connotes wealth and good social standing. The
word translated as Failure is* Kakotes *(more literally Badness); it
connotes poverty and bad social standing. The road to Failure is
easy because it demands no work.*

*It is apparently the thought that the wise man will take the road
to Success but the fool the road to Failure that leads to the descrip-
tion of the three different kinds of men. The best (among whom
Hesiod no doubt includes himself) are those who can see for them-
selves how things will turn out. Then there are those who are good
enough to take the advice of these wise ones; thus they are able to
learn without having to suffer like fools. Finally, there are the fools
(like Epimetheus) who neither know for themselves nor take the
advice of others who do. We can compare Proverbs 12:15: "A
fool thinks that he is always right; wise is the man who listens
to advice."*

*The reference to Perses' divine descent may be sarcastic, but it
may show that he and Hesiod claimed descent from the nobility of
Kyme. If so, it must have been difficult for them to adapt to their*

*lower social standing in Askra. Poverty and a low social standing
can be shameful; but Perses is advised not to try hiding his poverty
by not working.*

ADVICE ON BEING SUCCESSFUL

320 Gains not stolen but god-given turn out better by far.
For if one seizes great wealth for oneself by using sheer force
or gets plunder by means of one's tongue, as frequently
        happens
when the passion for gain deceives and befuddles the minds of
mortal men, and Shamelessness proves herself stronger than
        Shame,
325 easily he is abased by the gods, they ruin the house of
this sort of man, and he is but briefly prosperity's lord.
So too he is abased who harms suppliants, he who harms
        guest-friends,
he who goes up to lie in the bed where his brother should lie,
there to commit with his sister-in-law secret adultery,
330 he who in blindness of heart sins against fatherless children,
he who seeing his father in old age, in life's evil last days,
speaks to him harshly, reviling him roundly with words of
        abuse.
Zeus himself is undoubtedly angry with him and finally
makes him pay for his deeds of injustice a harsh retribution.
335 But keep your ruin-prone mind completely from thoughts of
        such deeds,
and make sacrifice to the immortals all that you can,
heart pure and hand pure; burn on their altars the glistening
        thigh bones,

and implore them at other times with libation and incense
both when you lie down to sleep and at the bright light of
     dawn,
340 so that their hearts and spirits may be propitious to you and
you may acquire the estate of others and not others yours.
Call your friend to your feast but leave your enemy out;
and invite him especially who lives in the house next to yours,
for if you have some misfortune befall you on your estate,
345 neighbors will come to you hastily dressed while kinsmen are
     dressing.
Bad neighbors plague us as much as good ones prosper us
     greatly.
He to whom a good neighbor is given is given a profit;
not one ox will he lose provided he has a good neighbor.
Fairly reckon the loan from your neighbor and fairly repay it,
350 using the very same measure, or better if you are able,
so that again being needy again you will find him supportive.
Get not gains that are evil; evil gains equal disaster.
Be a good friend to your friend and ready to help him
     approaching.
Give to him who is giving to you but not to him not giving.
355 Everyone gives to a giver; no one gives to a nongiver.
Giving is good but stealing is bad, a giver of death.
For when a man willingly gives and gives something large,
he receives joy of his gift and delight in his innermost soul;
but when he takes for himself what is not his, yielding to
     shamelessness,
360 although his theft is a small one, he causes the heart to freeze.
If you will add one small thing to another small thing, and
frequently do this, soon you will find that you have something
     large;
and he who adds to his stores will keep burning hunger away.

Nor does that which is stored on his homestead worry a man:
365 better keep it at home; what's out is a threatening bother.
It's a good thing to take from your own stores, a plague in the
    heart to
want what you don't have on hand; this I urge you to think of.
On opening and on finishing your storage jar take your desire,
but in the middle be sparing. Sparing is worst at the bottom.
370 See that the pay you have promised your man be given to
    him,
and when you deal with your brother laugh and call for a
    witness.
Surely trust no less than distrust brings ruin to men.
Let not a woman with buttocks attractively covered deceive
    you,
charmingly pleading and coaxing while poking into your
    barn.
375 He who trusts in women is putting his trust in deceivers.
May you have only one son to see that your ancestral
    homestead
has a provisioner, for so the wealth of your household will
    grow;
and may you die in old age with one son left to replace you.
Yet Zeus easily might bestow an abundance on more sons;
380 more will mean that the work done is greater and greater the
    profit.

COMMENT

*To be successful one must work and not steal. The thief is classified
with a number of other wrongdoers against whom Zeus takes ven-
geance. Another prerequisite of prosperity is the proper worship
of the gods. We can compare Psalm 37:9: "For evildoers will be
destroyed, but they who hope in the Lord shall possess the land."*

*One must also take care to have and keep good neighbors, and to
practice thrift and caution.*

THE FARMER'S CALENDAR

Introduction

If you want wealth, if that's what the heart in your breast
     desires,
do as I tell you to do and work with work upon work.
When you notice the daughters of Atlas, the Pleiades, rising,
start on your reaping, and on your sowing when they are
     setting.
385 They are hidden from view for a period of forty full days,
both night and day, but then once again, as the year moves
     round,
they reappear at the time for you to be sharpening your sickle.
The following law applies to the plainsmen, both to those who
dwell on the land near the sea and those who in upland valleys
390 far from the roaring surge of the sea, good country for farming,
have their abodes: strip to sow, strip to plow,
strip to reap. So do if you want to care for
all the works of Demeter each one in its season, that they
each may seasonably grow and you may not later be poor and
395 have to go begging at other men's houses and get no relief,
as even now you have come to me. But I shall not give you,
I shall not lend you anything more. Work, foolish Perses,
work at the works which the gods have granted to men as
     their portion,
so that you with your children and wife in distress may never
400 seek to subsist off the kindness of neighbors and find them
     unhelpful.

Twice or three times perhaps they will give, but bother them
         further
and you will get not a thing but make many speeches in vain
         and
useless will be your expansion of words. But do as I say and
plan your escape from impoverishment and your avoidance of
         hunger.

405 See that you have first of all a house, a woman, and a plow ox
(choose an unmarried slave woman fit to follow the oxen),
and prepare in your house for use whatever you'll need,
lest your request of another should fail and you be in want and
so the season will pass and your cultivation will suffer.

410 Don't put off what has to be done to tomorrow or next year,
for neither he who works ineffectively fills up his barn
nor he who puts off to act; attention prospers our work.
He who puts off his work is always wrestling with ruin.

COMMENT

*The Farmer's Calendar is mainly concerned with the production of
grain, which was the most important kind of wealth in Hesiod's
society. A man must work, and he must work in due season. Sowing
should begin when the Pleiades set (at the end of October), reaping
when they rise (during the second week in May). The time for
noting these signs is at dawn.*

*The exhortation to work stripped, or naked, no doubt means that
one should work with zeal, but perhaps it also means (so ancient
interpreters) that one should sow before the cold of winter comes
when clothing is necessary. We are later warned (479ff.) against
waiting until the solstice of winter to sow.*

*The man who neglects to work as he should, and also to make
necessary preparations, will have to beg from others, but they will
refuse to help him. We can compare Proverbs 20:4: "The sluggard
who does not plow in autumn goes begging at harvest and gets
nothing." We are given a picture of Perses begging with his wife*

*and children. Perhaps, as West suggests, he actually had no wife
and children, but they are added here to increase the pathos of the
scene; compare 270f., where Hesiod speaks as if he himself had a son.*

THE FARMER'S CALENDAR

Autumn

When the piercing strength of the sharp-rayed sun stops
415 burning with sweltering heat and the rains of autumn are
     poured by
  almighty Zeus from above and mortals experience the
     change,
  feeling much lighter in flesh, for Sirios, the scorching dogstar,
  passes by day for only a short time over the heads of
  doom-fated men and enjoys more of its journey at night,
420 then the wood you cut with your ax is least liable to worm,
  for it is shedding its leaves on the ground and ceasing to
     sprout.
  Then cut your wood, being mindful that this is the seasonable
     work.
  Cut out a mortar of three feet, a pestle of four and a half
     feet,
  and an axle of seven feet, much the best length for an axle;
425 if you have eight feet, you may cut off the head for a mallet.
  And cut a felly of three spans for a wagon of ten palms,
  many curved sections of wood. And bring the plowbeam you
     find
  back to your homestead, when you have searched the
     mountains and fields,
  one of the holm oak, for this is the strongest for oxen to plow
     with,

430 after the slave of Athena fixes it into the sharebeam,
      fitting it neatly with pegs, and fastens it onto the polebeam.
      See that you have two plows on your homestead ready for use,
      one single-pieced and one jointed, for it is much better thus:
      if one should break, you'll still have the other to hitch to your
            oxen.
435 Make your polebeams (to worms least exposed) of laurel or
            elm wood,
      and your sharebeams of oak and plowbeams of holm oak. And
            get two
      oxen of nine years, for then their strength, in the fullness of
            youth,
      isn't easily broken. These are the best ones to plow with;
      nor are they likely to fight in the furrow while plowing and
            cause your
440 plow to be broken and so leave the work then and there
            incomplete.
      And there should follow behind them a man in his fortieth
            year,
      having for dinner consumed a loaf of four quarters, eight
            pieces.
      He with his mind intent on his work will drive a straight
            furrow,
      no longer hankering to be with his comrades but keeping his
            thoughts on
445 what he is doing. Nor will a younger man be any better
      either at scattering the seed in the earth or not oversowing,
      for the man who is younger is fluttered to follow his comrades.
      Take careful note of the time when you hear the voice of the
            crane
      uttering high in the clouds her yearly trumpeting cry.
450 She announces the signal for plowing and points to the time of

winter and rain and vexes the heart of the man without oxen.
See to it then that you feed in their stalls your oxen of curved
     horn,
for it is easy to say, "Lend me your oxen and wagon,"
but a refusal is easy, "Sorry, my oxen are busy."
455 One says, rich in intent, that he will be building his wagon.
Fool, he knows not the truth that a wagon has one hundred
     planks,
which he should take care beforehand to see that he has on his
     homestead.
As soon as the time for plowing appears for mortal men,
you should set about doing your work, both you and your
     slave help,
460 plowing each day in dry earth and damp, the season for
     plowing,
starting at earliest dawn, so that your fields will be full.
Plow in the spring; fallow land plowed in the summer will
     prove true;
sow fallow land while still it is light to turn with your plow;
land that lies fallow nurses our children and keeps them from
     harm.
465 Pray to Zeus Chthonian and to the holy goddess Demeter
that the holy grain of Demeter will grow to fulfillment,
when you are first beginning to plow and have your plow
     handle
gripped in your hand and are using your switch on the backs
     of your oxen
and they are giving the strap pin a tug. Closely behind them
470 let a slave follow with mattock to create work for the birds by
hiding the seed in the earth. The best way for mortal men is
managing well; the worst way for them is managing badly.
Thus the full ears of grain will heavily nod to the ground,

if the Olympian himself afterward grants you fulfillment;
475 and you will clear your grain jars of cobwebs, and I expect
          that
     you will rejoice to take from the food you have in your
          storeroom,
     and you will come to the bright spring in plenty and not have
          to look to
     others for help, but others will look to you in their need.
     But should you wait for the solstice of winter to plow the
          divine earth,
480 you will reap sitting and gather only a small little handful,
     binding it crosswise, getting all dusty, not greatly rejoicing,
     and home you will bring it in only a basket and few will
          admire you.
     Yet now Zeus of the Aigis thinks this way, now he thinks that
          way;
     hard it is for mortal men to fathom his thinking.
485 So supposing you plow late still he may grant you this remedy:
     when the song of the cuckoo is heard from the leaves of the
          oak tree
     breaking forth for the first time and gladdening men on the
          broad earth,
     then Zeus may on the third day rain and rain without ceasing,
     not overreaching or underreaching the height of a bull's hoof.
490 Then plowing late may equal the worth of the earlier plowing.
     Guard these things all well in your heart and be not forgetful
     either of bright spring's arrival or of the season of rain.

COMMENT

*Autumn is not only the time for plowing and sowing but also for
cutting wood. Several wooden things are mentioned: the mortar and
pestle (for grinding the grain), the axle (for the wagon, used for*

carrying the seed corn to the field and for bringing in the harvest), and the mallet (used for breaking up the earth). The most important agricultural implements are the wagon (its fellies are also mentioned) and the plow. The jointed plow is described at some length; but we are also advised to have a simple curved piece of wood in reserve as a second plow. One naturally wonders why two jointed plows are not recommended. Perhaps, as Nicolai suggests, it is because of the expense of having to pay the carpenter (the slave of Athena) twice.

Half of a man's land should lie fallow each year, and there should be two earlier plowings, one in the spring and the other in the summer, before the autumn of the final plowing. In the picture of the beginning of plowing and sowing in autumn (465ff.), we are asked to visualize a procession of three men: first the plowman, then the sower, and finally a slave who covers the seed, preventing birds (like the crane mentioned in lines 448f.) from eating it. It seems likely that the farmer (and not the forty-year-old man recommended in lines 441ff.) is the plowman here because it is incumbent upon him to start things off religiously right by praying to Zeus and Demeter for the blessing of a good harvest. Zeus is given the epithet Chthonian because he is being addressed in his capacity as a god of the earth.

A man should sow in autumn; if he waits until the solstice of winter (in December) he will reap a very meager harvest. This is the general rule. But Hesiod, immediately after stating it, is struck by the pious thought that the mind of Zeus is unsearchable. If on the third day after the first cuckoo is heard (in March), Zeus rains so hard as exactly to fill up a bull's hoofprint (this seems the best interpretation of line 489), all will be well. We can compare the pious qualification of a general rule in lines 379f. and the alternative time to sail in lines 678ff.

THE FARMER'S CALENDAR

Winter

Pass by the blacksmith's forge and the warmth of its gathering
    place

during the freezing-cold weather of winter that keeps men
      from work
495 (then the diligent man can greatly prosper his homestead),
lest you be caught in the clutches of bad winter's helplessness
      and,

poverty-stricken, find that a thin hand squeezes a thick foot.
Often the shiftless man, relying on hopes that are empty,
lacking life's basic necessities, speaks evil words to his heart.
500 Hope, a bad kind of hope, attends on the needy man,
who with too little to live on haunts the gathering place.
Give your slaves this directive while still it's the middle of
      summer:

"Summer won't stay here forever and ever; be building the
      shelters."

And the month of Lenaion, evil days, bull-flayers all,
505 this you should try to avoid, and painful-to-slip-on ice slicks
which the wind of Boreas has hardened over the earth,
when he goes through the land of horse-breeding Thrace and
      blowing

stirs up the waves on the broad sea and sets earth and forest
      to howling.

Many a lofty leafy-topped oak tree and bulging-fat fir tree
510 up in the glens of the mountains he brings to the nourishing
      earth,

falling upon them, and everywhere then the thick forest is
      roaring.

And the animals shudder, their tails put under their legs;
even through them in spite of their skins that are covered
      with hair

he with his cold breath blows, in spite of their deep-shaggy
      breasts.

515 Through the hide of the ox he blows and isn't restrained,

and through the long-haired pile of the goat. Yet powerful
    Boreas
isn't able to blow through the sheep, whose fleece by now has
grown to abundance; but he makes the old man a runner.
And he's unable to blow through the delicate skin of the
    young girl,
520 who in the safety of home stays by her dear mother's side,
being as yet without knowledge of Aphrodite the Golden.
She after bathing her soft skin well and anointing herself with
rich olive oil lies down to rest in her corner within doors
during the winter's day, while the Boneless One gnaws at his
    own foot
525 where he inhabits a house without fire and a cheerless abode,
for now the sun does not light him the way to a pasture to
    head for,
but is holding his course over the people and city of
black-skinned men and shining more tardily on the
    Panhellenes.
Then the horned and the hornless, creatures that dwell in the
    forest,
530 piteously chattering, moaning, try to escape up through
the tree-covered glens—this is the care in each of their
    minds—
into those places they seek when wanting protection, their
    close lairs
deep in the rocks. Then they resemble the three-legged
    mortal
who has a back that is broken and head looking down to the
    ground;
535 like him they hurry along, avoiding the white falling snow.
Then you should see that your skin is protected as I advise you
both by a good soft coat and a chiton extending full length.

Take care to weave, on a warp that is light, a woof that is
heavy;
this is the cloth you should wear to prevent your trembling
hair from
540 standing up straight in a bristle, rising all over your body.
And on your feet bind boots of the hide of a slaughtered ox,
fitting them closely, when you have cushioned their insides
with felt.

And when the season of frost comes, sew together with ox gut
skins of the newborn kid to throw on your back as a covering
545 so as to ward off the rain. And put a cap on your head,
one that is well made of felt, to protect your ears from the wet.
For it is cold when Boreas is starting to blow at dawn
and when the mist is poured at dawn down over the earth
out of the star-studded sky on the wheat-bearing lands of the
blessed.
550 This mist, drawn up from the streams of ceaselessly flowing
rivers
and raised high in the sky over earth by the blast of the wind,
sometimes returns as rain in the evening, sometimes in dark
gusts,
when the thick clouds are driven in confusion by Thracian
Boreas.
Keeping ahead of him finish your work and return to your
homestead,
555 lest descending from heaven the black cloud cover you over,
making your flesh to feel clammy and giving your clothing a
soaking.
See that you try to avoid him, for this is the hardest of months,
wintry and stormy, hard on the livestock, hard on us humans.
Then give half to your oxen, but more than half to your man,
of

560 usual rations, for long are the helpful well-disposed times.
   Observing this rule see that you make the nights balance the
        days
   until the year has come to fulfillment and once again
   earth, the mother of all, produces her manifold crops.

COMMENT

*Winter is no time to be loitering in the warm shop of the black-
smith, where men were accustomed to gather as in the modern coffee-
house. The man who is unprepared with sufficient food and clothing
will "find that a thin hand squeezes a thick foot." Hesiod is no doubt
thinking of hunger as well as cold and frostbite, for other ancient
authors describe swollen feet as a symptom of starvation.*

*We are given a vivid description of Lenaion, the hardest month
of winter (during January and February). It is characterized in
terms of the north wind Boreas. The blessed condition of the young
girl at home is contrasted with that of the Boneless One (a riddling
expression, probably for the octopus which eats its own tentacles).
The fleeing animals are compared to the three-legged mortal (the old
man with a cane). As Nicolai points out, the making of winter
clothes is described here not only because the farmer has time to make
them now but also because this is the time when they are especially
needed. We should compare the description of the making of farm
tools in the section on autumn.*

*In winter oxen should receive only half of their usual rations,
and men only somewhat more than half, because they are working
less. The expression "well-disposed times" is a euphemism for nights.
The final exhortation to "make the nights balance the days" means
that one should increase rations with the increasing length of the
days until the time of new harvest in spring.*

THE FARMER'S CALENDAR

Spring and Summer

   But when Zeus has brought to fulfillment the sixty-day period
565 after the solstice of winter, a period of stormy weather,

then the star Arkturos, leaving sacred Okeanos,
brightly shines for the first time in evening's earliest darkness.
Next the swallow, the lamenting child of Pandion, appears,
coming into the sight of men when spring is beginning.

570 Keeping ahead of her, prune your vines, for this will be better.
But when the House Carrier goes up onto the plants from the
    earth,
fleeing the Pleiades, then no longer be hoeing your vines,
but be sharpening your sickles and rousing your slaves to their
    work.
Flee the seat in the shade and staying in bed until dawn

575 during the season of reaping when the sun is withering the
    flesh.
This is the time to be hastening and bringing your harvest
    home,
rising at daybreak, that you may have sufficient to live on.
For Dawn rightfully claims as her own a third of the day's
    work;
Dawn gives a man a start on the road and a start on his work,

580 Dawn that brightly arising stirs up many a man to
go on his way and sets the yoke upon many an ox team.
But when you see the scolymus flowering and hear the cicada
sing in the tree, sending its beautiful, vibrating song
pulsing from under its wings in the season of scorching-hot
    summer,

585 then you will find that she-goats are fattest, wine most
    delicious,
women most desirous of love but men most enfeebled,
for now the dogstar Sirios parches their heads and their knees,
and in the heat their skin becomes dry. Then would I have
a shady retreat in the cool of the rocks, and Bibline wine with

590 milk-leavened bread and milk of goats that are starting to go
    dry,

and meat of cow that has fed in the woods, one never in calf,
and

that of the newborn kid. And then would I drink of the red
wine,

as I relax in the shade, my appetite sated completely,

turning my face to enjoy the cooling breezes of Zephyros,

595 and would pour from a clear and ever free-flowing stream

three parts of water to mix for my drink with one part of wine.

But as soon as the strength of Orion arises, you should

urge your slaves to thresh the holy grain of Demeter

on a spot well swept by the wind, well leveled for threshing.

600 Then you should measure it off well into your jars. But when
you've

got your supply all safely stored on your homestead within
doors,

find as hired laborers to help you a man without home and a
woman,

one without child, I advise you, for one with a child is a
burden.

And take care of your sharp-toothed dog, don't stint on his
rations,

605 lest the Day Sleeper come and steal away your goods.

And you should bring in fodder and litter so that there'll be

plenty enough for your oxen and mules. And then it is time to

grant your slaves a rest for their legs and your oxen their
freedom.

But when the stars of Orion and Sirios have climbed up into

610 midheaven and rosy-fingered Dawn is facing Arkturos,

then, Perses, pluck and bring home all your clusters of grapes.

Set them to dry in the heat of the sun for ten days and nights,

and in the shade for five days, and then on the sixth day
draw off

the blessings of glad Dionysos into your jars. But when you
615 notice that the Pleiades and the Hyades and the strength of
        Orion are setting,
then is the time for you to be mindful of plowing again,
acting in season, and let the seed duly be sowed in the earth.

COMMENT

*We are given advice on viticulture as well as on grain growing.
Vines should be hoed and pruned before the rising of Arkturos in
the evening sky sixty days after the solstice of winter (during the
third week in February) and before the coming of the swallow (later
in February). The swallow is referred to as the "child of Pandion"—
an allusion to the myth that the daughter of this Athenian king,
after her brother-in-law Tereus had raped her and cut out her
tongue, was metamorphosed into this bird. The time for harvesting
the grain is signaled when the House Carrier (the snail) climbs
onto the plants (probably the vines) to escape the heat that comes
with the rising of the Pleiades (during the second week in May).*

*When Orion is seen to rise at dawn (in the latter half of June),
the grain, which will have dried out and ripened in the husks, should
be threshed and stored in jars. Now is the time to hire new servants
for the coming year and to feed one's watchdog well to make him
fit to frighten off the Day Sleeper (the thief). The grapes should be
picked when Orion and Sirios have come into midheaven and Ark-
turos is rising at dawn (about the middle of September), and then,
after a fifteen-day period for further ripening, should be pressed into
wine, which should be stored in its jars.*

*Hesiod interrupts this advice on viticulture and grain growing
with a passage in which he describes a refreshing vacation from
work in the heat of summer. The signs for this vacation are the
flowering of the scolymus (the golden thistle) and the singing of
the cicada (in the latter half of June) and the rising of Sirios at
dawn (toward the end of July). Hesiod's idyllic picture is evidence
that he was no puritan who believed in work for work's sake. It
is imitated by the lyric poet Alkaios in one of his drinking poems.
All the food and drink is choice; the wine, for instance, is a good*

Bibline, probably so called from the name of a place in Thrace. But one is struck by the loneliness of the scene: a loaf of bread, a jug of wine, but no thou. Women are dismissed with the witticism that their sexual craving in the hot time of summer ill sorts with the dried-up condition of men.

The Farmer's Calendar ends as it begins with an address to Perses, and we are given a fullness of signs announcing the coming of autumn and the time to plow and sow again. The year has come full circle.

A GUIDE FOR THE MERCHANT SAILOR.
HESIOD'S WITNESS

But if you are desirous of trying tempestuous sailing,
when the Pleiades flee the mighty strength of Orion
620 and begin to descend into the shadowy deep,
then the wild winds are blowing and rushing from every
        direction,
and you should no longer keep your ship on the wine-dark
        sea,
but be mindful of doing your farmwork as I advise you.
Draw your ship onto the shore and prop her up neatly with
        stones
625 everywhere round to stand in the force of the damp-blowing
        winds,
pulling the bilge plug, lest she rot in the Zeus-sent rain.
And store all your sailing equipment safely at home,
putting in excellent order the wings of your seagoing ship,
and hang your well-crafted rudder above in the smoke of your
        fireplace.
630 So you should wait for the seasonable time for sailing to come.
Then you may draw your swift ship into the water and load
        her

carefully with cargo that you may come home again with a
        profit,
sailing just as my father and yours, Perses, you great fool,
kept on sailing in ships, seeking a prosperous living.
635 Once he came even here in his black ship when he had crossed
a broad stretch of sea and left behind him Kyme in Aiolis,
not fleeing wonderful plenty or wealth and blessed good
        fortune
but the curse of starvation, an evil Zeus sends upon men.
And he settled in Askra, a miserable village near Helikon,
640 which is a bad place in winter, a hard one in summer, good
        never.
But you, Perses, I beg you, be mindful of doing your work,
every work in its season, but take thought especially of sailing.
Praise the ship that is small but put your load in a large one,
for the greater the load the greater the gain upon gain
645 coming to you, if only the winds don't blow you destruction.
Should you choose to escape from your debts and mirth-
        destroying
hunger by turning your ruin-prone mind to being a merchant,
let me show you the rules of the loud-roaring sea to follow,
though I completely lack any training in ships or in sailing,
650 for never yet have I sailed across the broad sea in a ship
except for my trip to Euboia from Aulis, where the Achaioi
waited the storm out with the great army they'd gathered to
        sail from
Hellas the holy to fight against Troy of the beautiful women.
Here I myself embarked for the games of noble Amphidamas
655 and for the city of Chalkis, the sons of this great man having
promised to give many prizes. There I can boast that I won
as the victor in song an ear-handled tripod-cauldron,
which I then set up as a gift to the Muses of Helikon
where they first made me start on the way of beautiful singing.

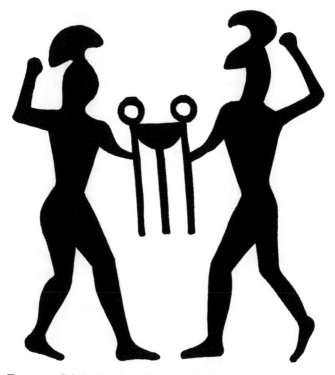

Two men fighting over a tripod-cauldron—from a scene in low relief on the leg of a tripod-cauldron of the late eighth century B.C. *in the Olympia Museum, Olympia, Greece; compare* W.D. *656ff.*

660 This is all the experience I have of many-pegged ships,
  but even so I shall tell you the mind of Zeus of the Aigis,
  for the Muses have taught me to sing and inspired me with
      song.
  There is a fifty-day period after the solstice of summer,
  the scorching-hot season of summer having come to
      fulfillment,
665 when it is seasonable for mortals to sail, and you would neither
  shatter your ship nor lose any men in the gulf of the sea,
  if Poseidon the Shaker of Earth not show his disfavor
  or Zeus the King of the Gods not want to grant you
      destruction,
  for in their power is fulfillment alike of good things and bad.
670 During this time the breezes are steady and safe is the sea.
  Then entrusting your swift ship to the winds with a confident
      spirit,
  draw her down into the water and put all your cargo aboard,
  and as quickly as possible hasten to come home again.
  Don't delay to the time of the new wine and the late autumn
      rainstorms
675 and the approach of winter and the terrible blowing of Notos,
  who sets the sea in a stir and causes the water to roughen,
  working in concert with Zeus who sends the great autumn
      rains.
  But spring is another possible time for men to sail.
  Just as soon as a man first sees the leaves of the fig tree
680 barely sprouting to life, being as small as the footprint
  left by the crow on the earth, then he may put out to sea.
  This is the time for sailing in spring. I for my part
  give it no good word, for it displeases me in my heart.
  It's something stolen, and you'll hardly escape from
      destruction.

685 But men will sail at this time because of their blindness of
           mind,
     for the possession of wealth means life to poor human beings.
     It's a terrible thing to die in the waves. So I am urging you
     that you should ponder deep in your heart all my advice.
     Don't entrust to hollow ships the whole of your livelihood,
690 but keep the greater part out and load on the smaller part,
     for it's a terrible thing to meet with disaster at sea;
     and it's a terrible thing if by overloading your wagon
     you should shatter its axle and ruin what you are carrying.
     Carefully keep to due measure; what's fitting in all things is
           best.

COMMENT

*Sailing is the means by which the farmer can sell his produce over-
seas, but it is a dangerous enterprise and demands the greatest cau-
tion. We begin by being told not to sail when we should be plowing
and sowing in autumn. The best time to sail is during the fifty-
day period after the summer solstice (from June 22 through August
11). But Hesiod also mentions another time, which he considers a
very bad second, in spring after the first leaves are seen on the fig
tree (during the latter half of April).*

*By way of expounding these rules and explaining his knowledge
of them, he gives us important information about himself and his
family. This is discussed more fully in the Introduction. His knowl-
edge of sailing comes from the Muses, for he has never sailed farther
than from Aulis to Chalkis (about seventy yards), where he won
the tripod-cauldron at the funeral games of Amphidamas.*

*We are advised not only about the right time to sail but also
about the proper loading of our cargo. A big ship is better than a
small one because it holds more, but we must beware of putting
all our goods in one ship. Similarly, we must beware of overloading
our wagon—a more necessary warning for the farmer to heed,
which leads to the generalization that due measure in all things is*

best. We remember that the wagon, unlike the ship, is one of the
farmer's essential implements; compare 434ff. and 455ff.

SOCIAL AND RELIGIOUS ADVICE

695 At the seasonable time bring home a wife for yourself,
   when you are just about thirty, not being many years younger
   or being many years older, for this is the best time to marry.
   Let a woman mature for four years and be married the fifth
         year.
   And you should marry a virgin that you may teach her to act
         right,

700 and especially one who lives in a house near to yours,
   looking all round, lest your marriage should give your
         neighbors amusement.
   For a man gets to possess nothing better at all than a wife,
   if she is good, nothing more horrible if she is bad,
   if she's a gluttonous woman who roasts her husband without
         fire,

705 withering him, though he's a strong man, prematurely to old
         age.
   Carefully reverence the blessed immortals and guard against
         vengeance.
   Don't be granting a friend the equality due to a brother;
   but should you do so, don't be the first to harm him in deed
   or by belying your tongue's gracious speech. But if he first
         should

710 say to you something not in his heart or do you some wrong,
   be of set mind to pay him back doubly. But if again he
   asks for your friendship and shows a willingness to make
         compensation,

give him your welcome. He is a bad man who takes as his
     friend
now this one, now that one. Let your appearance reflect your
     intention.
715 Neither be called a popular friend nor a man who is friendless,
nor a companion of bad men nor a taunter of good men.
Never dare to blame a man for soul-destroying
poverty's curse, for this is the gift of the blessed immortals.
It is the tongue that is best of all the treasures men cherish,
720 if it is sparing, and greatest grace shines from it temperately
     moving.
If you speak evil, soon you will hear greater evil yourself.
Don't be speaking with boisterous ease at a large dinner party;
there you will win greatest grace by expending your treasure
     least.
Never pour at dawn libation of red wine to Zeus
725 or to the other immortals before you have washed your hands,
for if you do they will not pay attention but spit back your
     prayers.
Don't stand up and make water facing the light of the sun;
and in the time between sunset and sunrise see that you don't
urinate while you are walking on or off the road,
730 nor be showing your nakedness, for the nights belong to the
     blessed ones;
and the man who is god-fearing and knows what is right will
     sit
or withdraw to one of the walls of a well-enclosed courtyard.
Nor be displaying yourself with your private parts covered
     with semen
near your hearth at home; you should avoid doing this.
735 Nor when you've just returned from a funeral, an ill-omened
     matter,
should you engage in begetting, but after a feast of the gods.

Don't ever cross on foot the ceaselessly flowing streams of
beautiful rivers before you have prayed, looking into their
     brightness,
with your hands washed clean in their much-loved sparkling
     water.
740 He who crosses a river with hands unwashed of their evil
earns from the gods disapproval and later a painful requital.
Nor cut off the dry from the green of the five-branched thing
with the glittering iron at a bountiful feast of the gods.
Nor ever set the wine ladle on the top of the wine bowl
745 when you are drinking, for this will entail a terrible fate.
Nor should you leave a house you're building with uneven
     planks,
lest the loud-crying crow should settle upon it and caw.
Nor should you draw from a cauldron that isn't properly
     blessed
water for meal or for bath, for also in this there's a penalty.
750 Nor should you set on immovable things—better not do
     this—
him who is twelve days old, for men are made impotent thus;
or him twelve months of age, which entails the same bad
     effect.
Nor should a man dare to wash his flesh in the water already
used by a woman, for this too exacts for a time a grievous
755 penalty from him. Nor when you've come on men making
     burnt sacrifice
find any fault with their offering, for this too displeases a god.
Nor ever urinate either into seaward-flowing rivers
or into springs, but see that you greatly avoid doing this;
nor be relieving yourself, for this too is not better for you.
760 Thus you should do, and avoid a dread reputation among
     men.
For a bad reputation, though it's very easy to pick up,

since it's a light thing, is painful to carry and hard to get rid of.
No reputation dies out completely once there are many
people reporting it; and so Reputation is also a god.

COMMENT

*We are first advised on the right time to marry. The woman should
be about eighteen (five years past puberty). A man should take care
to marry a woman who will not make him a laughingstock (prob-
ably as a cuckold) among the neighbors. A good wife is the best of
possessions, but a bad one will destroy her husband. We can compare
Proverbs 12:4: "A capable wife is her husband's crown; one who
disgraces him is like rot in his bones."*

*The exhortation in line 706 to guard against the vengeance of the
gods comes somewhat unexpectedly, but perhaps we should connect it
with the idea of avoiding a bad reputation, which is important both
in the preceding lines and in those that follow on friendship and
temperate speech. The tongue should be used sparingly and wisely.
The poor are not to be blamed for their poverty; this is a gift of
the gods. We can compare Proverbs 17:5: "A man who sneers at
the poor insults his Maker, and he who gloats over another's ruin
will answer for it."*

*Lines 724–59 give a list of religious prohibitions or taboos. The
prohibition not to "cut off the dry from the green of the five-branched
thing" refers to the fingernails. The "immovable things" upon which
we are forbidden to set a male baby are tombstones. These prohibi-
tions are often denied to Hesiod on the ground that they seem incon-
sistent with the rational thinking he elsewhere displays. But it is
easy to see how he may have come to include them. Men who are
god-fearing and for the most part rational have often been bound by
such superstitions.*

*Finally, we are given an exhortation to avoid a bad reputation.
This is described in terms that sound like the adaptation of a riddle.
What is easy to pick up, painful to carry, and hard to get rid of?
Reputation can be counted as a divinity because it lives on and on.*

THE *DAYS*

765 Observing the Zeus-sent days and keeping them well in due
        order,
    point out to your slaves that the thirtieth day of the month is
        best
    both for assessing the work and making division of rations,
    when men discerning the truth observe this day at the right
        time.
    The following days are those that are sent by Zeus of the
        Counsels.
770 First, the first and the fourth are holy, and also the seventh
    (for on this day Leto gave birth to gold-sworded Apollo),
    and the eighth and the ninth. But there are two days of the
        month that
    when it is waxing especially benefit men in their work:
    the eleventh and twelfth, for these are truly good days both for
775 shearing the sheep and for gathering the gladdening grain.
    But of the two the twelfth is the one that is better by far,
    for on this day the high-flying spider spins his fine thread,
    starting at full day, and then the Wise One gathers her heap.
    Then a woman should set up her loom and work at her
        weaving.
780 But on the thirteenth day, when the month is beginning, avoid
    sowing your seed; this time is best for putting out plants.
    Very unsuited for plants is the middle sixth day of the month;
    yet for a boy's birth good, but again unsuited for girls
    either for birth in the first place or for their entry on marriage.
785 Nor is the first sixth day a time for the birth of a girl,
    but you will find it for gelding the kids and the sheep of the
        flock
    and for enclosing a fold for the sheep a favorable day.

This day is good for a boy's birth, but he will like to jeer and
lie and speak wheedling words and whispers in confidence.
790 The eighth of the month is the time when the hog and the
            roaring bull
ought to be gelded, but on the twelfth the hardworking mules.
On the great twentieth day in the fullness of midday a wise
            man
ought to be born, for he will be blessed with a close-thinking
            mind.
Good for the birth of a boy is the tenth, the fourth for a girl
795 when it is midmonth. Then sheep and shambling oxen of
            curved horn
and the sharp-toothed dog and the hardworking mule ought
            to be
gently tamed to the touch of your hand. But be on your
            guard,
both when the month is waning and waxing, on fourth days,
            lest you
suffer some painful result, for this day especially is fateful.
800 But on the fourth of the month you should bring home a wife
            for yourself,
after observing the birds that are best for taking this action.
Fifths are days to avoid because of their hardness and terror,
for on a fifth we are told the Erinyes attended the birth of
the oath-god Horkos, that plague to perjurers mothered by
            Eris.
805 And on the seventh of the midmonth, being careful of what
            you are doing,
on a well-rounded threshing place you should toss up
the holy grain of Demeter; and the woodsman should cut
            wood for
building a house and many good planks for building a ship.

And on the fourth day see that you start to construct a slim
   ship.

810 The afternoon of the ninth of the midmonth proves to be
   better,

but the first ninth is freest of pain for mortal men,

for it is good both for putting out plants and having a child,

whether a male or a female, and never wholly a bad day.

But few know that the triple ninth day of the month is the
   best for

815 opening a jar and for putting the neck of the oxen

and of the mules and the swift-footed horses under the yoke,

and for starting to draw the swift and many-oared ship

into the wine-dark sea; few call this day by its true name.

Open a jar on the fourth day, which is the holiest of days

820 when it is midtime. Few know that the day that comes after
   the twentieth

while it is morning is best but worse in the afternoon.

These are the days that especially benefit men on the earth.

The others are changeable, lacking in character, bearers of
   nothing.

Men praise various days, but few of them do so with
   knowledge.

825 Sometimes a day resembles a stepmother, sometimes a mother.

In his days happy and blessed is he who knows all this

and so works as not to offend the immortal gods,

being observant of omens of birds and avoiding transgressions.

COMMENT

The authenticity of the Days *has been questioned on several grounds,
the most important being its superstitious character and the fact
that it gives advice which must have sometimes been in conflict
with that given earlier in* W.D. *For instance, the belief that the*

eleven and twelfth of the month are especially good for reaping must have sometimes conflicted with the rule that this should be done at the rising of the Pleiades. But the superstitious character of the Days *shows it to belong to the same world as the religious prohibitions of the preceding section (see the Comment there); and the conflict between a rational and a superstitious rule for the same activity has not prevented other societies from accepting them both.*

It seems likely that Hesiod's account of the days is indebted to foreign influence, for he sometimes describes them in the same way as the Mesopotamians and the Egyptians do: by their connection with some god or as consisting of two or three parts of different effect. The case for Mesopotamian influence is stronger, as West notes, because Hesiod agrees with the Assyrians against the Egyptians in not distinguishing between months.

We begin with an exhortation that strikes a practical, rational note. We are told to assess the work of our slaves and apportion their rations on the last day of the month, that is, the thirtieth.

There are three main ways of counting the days: consecutively from the first to the thirteenth; according to whether a day occurs in the first, second, or third decad of the month; and according to whether a day belongs to the waxing or waning half of the month. Since beginnings are fraught with danger, the wise man will know the best day for every new undertaking. For instance, the twelfth is good for gathering the grain and for starting to weave, because on it the spider starts to weave his web and the Wise One (the ant) gathers her heap. The only days that are completely bad are fifths (probably the fifth of each decad), the reason being that on this day Eris (the bad Strife) gave birth to Horkos.

We end by being told to observe the signs of birds; compare 801. Belief in divination by birds was common in Hesiod's time as well as in later antiquity; and a poem on this subject, the Divination by Birds, *for which we have only the title, was attributed to him and appended to* W.D.

Select Bibliography

TEXTS, COMMENTARIES, AND TRANSLATIONS

Brown, N. O. *Hesiod's Theogony,* New York, 1953. English translation with introduction.

Butler, S. *Works and Days,* London, 1924. English translation.

Colonna, A. *Hesiodi Opera et Dies,* Milan, 1959. Edition.

Evelyn-White, H. G. *Hesiod, the Homeric Hymns and Homerica* (Loeb series), London, 1914, revised 1920 and 1936, reprinted 1964. Greek text and English translation.

Lattimore, R. *Hesiod,* Ann Arbor, 1959, English translation.

Mair, A. W. *Hesiod, The Poems and Fragments,* Oxford, 1908. English translation with valuable commentary on farmer's calendar and agricultural implements.

Marg, W. *Hesiod: Sämtliche Gedichte,* Stuttgart, 1970. German translation and commentary.

Mazon, P. *Hésiode, Les Travaux et les Jours,* Paris, 1914. Greek text and commentary.

——. *Hésiode: Theogonie, Les Travaux et les Jours, Le Bouclier* (Budé series), Paris, 1928, reprinted 1960. Greek text and French translation.

Rowe, C. J. *Essential Hesiod,* Bristol, 1978. Greek text of select passages with introduction and notes.

Rzach, A. *Hesiodi Carmina,* Leipzig, 1913, reprinted with additions, Stuttgart, 1967. Edition.

Sinclair, T. A. *Hesiod: Works and Days,* London, 1932, reprinted Hildesheim, 1966. Greek text and commentary.

Solmsen, F. *Hesiodi Theogonia, Opera et Dies, Scutum,* Oxford, 1970. Edition.

Wender, D. *Hesiod: Theogony, Works and Days; Theognis: Elegies,* Harmondsworth, 1973. English translation.

West, M. L. *Hesiod: Theogony,* Oxford, 1966. Edition and commentary.

———. *Hesiod: Works and Days,* Oxford, 1978. Edition and commentary.

Wilamowitz-Moellendorff, U. von. *Hesiodos Erga,* Berlin, 1928, reprinted 1962. Greek text and commentary.

BOOKS AND ARTICLES

Bona Quaglia, L. *Gli "Erga" di Esiodo,* Turin, 1973.

Burn, A. R. *The World of Hesiod,* London, 1936.

Edwards, G. P. *The Language of Hesiod in its Traditional Context,* Oxford, 1971.

Fränkel, H. *Dichtung und Philosophie des frühen Griechentums,* 2nd ed., Munich, 1962, chap. 3; translated by M. Hadas and J. Willis, Oxford, 1975.

Fontenrose, J. *Python,* Berkeley and Los Angeles, 1959.

Groningen, B. A. van. *La Composition Littéraire Archaïque Grecque,* 2nd ed., Amsterdam, 1960, esp. pp. 256–303.

Heitsch, E. *Hesiod (Wege der Forschung,* 44), Darmstadt, 1966. A collection of articles by various scholars.

Krafft, F. *Vergleichende Untersuchungen zu Homer und Hesiod,* Göttingen, 1963.

Kumaniecki, K. "The Structure of Hesiod's Works and Days," *Bulletin of Institute of Classical Studies* 10 (1963):79–96.

Minton, W. W. "The Proem-Hymn of Hesiod's Theogony," *Transactions and Proceedings of the American Philological Association* 101 (1970):357–77.

Nicolai, W. *Hesiods Erga: Beobachtungen zum Aufbau,* Heidelberg, 1964.

Solmsen, F. *Hesiod and Aeschylus,* Ithaca, 1949.

Verdenius, W. J. "Aufbau und Absicht der *Erga,*" in *Hésiode et son Influence (Entretiens sur L'Antiquité Classique,* 7), Geneva, 1960, pp. 111–59.

Walcot, P. *Hesiod and the Near East,* Cardiff, 1966.

Index

Achilleus (Achilles): 13, 89

Aietes, father of Medeia: 87, 89

Aineias (Aeneas): 89, 90

Aison, father of Iason: 89

Alkmene, mother of Herakles: 87

Amphidamas, at whose funeral games Hesiod won tripod-cauldron: 4–6, 60, 131, 134

Amphitrite: daughter of Nereus, 41; wife of Poseidon, 86

Aphrodite: 23, 34, 36–38, 40, 56, 80, 86–90, 98, 124

Apollo: 23; inspirer of singers, 27, 29; nurse of men, 48–49; birth of, 85, 139

Ares: 59, 85–86

Artemis: 23, 85

Athena (Tritogeneia): 23; counselor of Herakles, 45; dresser of first woman (Pandora), 65–67, 98–99; birth of, 83–86; carpenter, slave of, 119, 122

Atlas, son of Iapetos: holds up sky, 61–64, 75; father of Maia, 87; father of Pleiades, 116

Bellerophon, slayer of Chimaira: 45, 47

Bible, quotations from: *Prov. 26:27*, 11; *Ps. 96:6*, 53; *Ps. 97:3–4*, 74; *Ps. 74:12–14*, 83; *1 Sam. 2:6–7*, 93–94; *Ps. 37: 16*, 97; *Prov. 12:15*, 112; *Ps. 37:9*, 115; *Prov. 20:4*, 117; *Prov. 12:4*, 138; *Prov. 17:5*, 138

Chaos: 14, 30, 72, 77

Cheiron, the centaur: 89

Demeter: birth of, 56, 59; mother of Persephone, 84; mother of Ploutos, 88; goddess of grain, 96, 111, 116, 120, 122, 128, 140

Dionysos: birth of, 87, 90; married to Ariadne, 87; god of wine, 129

Echidna, the monster who mates with Typhoeus: 44–47

Eileithyia, the goddess of childbirth: 59, 85

Eos (Dawn), the Early Born: 24,

128; mother of the winds (Boreas, Notos, and Zephyros) and of the stars, 50–52; other children of, 88; praised by Hesiod, 127

Erinys, Erinyes (Fury, Furies): arise from blood of Ouranos, 36–37, 39, 57, 59; attendants at birth of Horkos, 140

Eris (Strife): good and bad, 4, 13, 40, 86, 94–97; the bad, 39–40, 105, 140

Eros: birth of, 30; attends upon Aphrodite, 37; motivating force in *Theog.*, 97

Etymologies, of names such as: Kalliope, 29; Aphrodite, 36; Nereus, 40; Okeanos, 43, 50; Pegasos, 44; Hekate, 56

Eurynome: daughter of Okeanos, 48, 50; mother of the Graces, 84

Failure *(Kakotes):* 111–12

Fate of man, determined by the creation of woman (Pandora): 64–68, 97–100; *see also* Moirai

Gaia (Earth): 24–25, 28, 30, 32–37, 40, 47, 54, 61, 126; prophecies of, 57, 69, 71, 83–84; nurse of Zeus, 58; mother of Typhoeus, 80–82; original parent of gods and men, 104

Giants: 25, 36–37, 71

Gorgons: 43, 46

Graces: 26, 29, 98

Graiai (Gray Ones): 43, 46

Hades (God of the Under-world): birth of, 56, 59; house of, 76, 102; is frightened, 81; rapes Persephone, 84

Harpies: 43

Hebe (Youth): daughter of Hera, 59, 85; wife of Herakles, 87

Hekate: 52–56

Helen, the cause of the Trojan War: 103

Hephaistos (Lame-Legged One): creator of first woman (Pandora), 65–67, 98; god of fire, 82; birth of, a counter miracle to Athena's birth, 85–86; husband of youngest Grace, 87

Hera: 23, 37; enemy of Herakles, 45–46; birth of, 56, 59; children of, 85

Herakles: monster-slayer, 44–47, 63–64, 88; birth and deification of, 87

Hermes (Slayer of Argos): birth of, 87, 90; helps in the making of Pandora and names her, 98–99

Hesiod: 3–8, 10–18; his dispute with Perses, 5, 96–97; forerunner of earliest philosophers, 14; compared with Homer, 16–17; mentions himself by name, 24; his description of a summer vacation, 129–30; winner of the tripod-cauldron, 131

Hesperides: birth of, 38; the golden apples of, 46–47; Atlas stands before, 63

Hestia: 56, 59

Hope: left in the jar, 99–100;

bad kind of, 123
Horai (Hours or Seasons): birth of, 84, 86; help to dress Pandora, 98; *see also* Justice
Horkos, the oath-god: born of the bad Eris, 39-40, 96, 140; pursues injustice, 108
Hundred-Handers, who help Zeus against the Titans: 33-34, 61, 68-75, 78
Hybris: defined, 14; in Story of Ages of Man, 102-105; no match for Justice, 106-11
Hydra, monster slain by Herakles: 45-47
Hymns and hymnic structure: 23-28, 38, 56, 93

Iapetos: birth of, 32; sons of, 61-67, 75
Iason (Jason), son of Aison and husband of Medeia: 89
Iolaos, assistant of Herakles: 45
Iris: birth of, 42-43; fetches water of Styx for Zeus, 76

Justice *(Dike)*: of great importance to Hesiod, 10-12, 14; one of the three Horai, 84-86; triumphs over Hybris, 106-11

Kadmos: daughters of, 87-88; Thebes, the city of, 103
Kerberos (Cerberus), the dog of Hades: 45-46, 76
Kronos: 8-9, 16, 24, 33; castrates Ouranos, 34-38; swallows his children, 56-60; in Tartaros, 81; king of heaven during the time of

the golden race, 101, 105
Kyklopes (Cyclopes), who make the thunderbolts for Zeus: 9, 33-34, 59-61

Leto, mother of Apollo and Artemis: 53, 55, 85, 139

Medeia (Medea): 88, 89
Medusa: 44
Metis (Wisdom): daughter of Okeanos, 48; mother of Athena by Zeus, 83-86
Mnemosyne (Memory), mother of the Muses: 25, 29, 32, 84
Moirai (Fates): 13; two parentages of, 14; daughters of Night, 38-39; daughters of Zeus and Themis, 84, 86
Muses: 5, 15, 88, 90; frequenters of Mount Helikon and inspirers of Hesiod, 3-4, 12, 23-30, 131, 133; names of, 14, 17, 26-27, 29; born in Pieria and called Pierian, 25, 93-94

Nemesis: daughter of Night, 38; will abandon men of the iron race, 104-105
Nereus and his daughters: 40-42, 89
Night: 24, 30, 32, 43, 74; progeny of, 38-40, 105; house of, 75-76, 78

Odysseus (Ulysses): 89, 90
Oidipous (Oedipus): 7, 47, 103
Okeanos, daughters of: 41-42, 44, 61, 76-77, 84, 87-88

Pandora: 11, 40, 97–100

Pegasos: fetches thunderbolts for Zeus, 44; helps Bellerophon, 45

Persephone, daughter of Demeter raped by Hades: 84

Perses (1), Hesiod's brother: his dispute with Hesiod, 5, 96–97; divine descent of, 5, 111–12; pictured as fool, 10, 12; *W.D.* addressed to, 93, 96, 111, 116, 128, 131; wife and children of, 116–18

Perses (2), father of Hekate: 51–53, 55

Perseus, slayer of Medusa: 44, 47

Ploutos (Wealth), son of Demeter: 88

Poseidon: Shaker of Earth, 23, 54, 57, 59, 133; He of the Black Mane, 44, 46; built door of Tartaros, 75; father-in-law of Hundred-Hander, 78; father of Triton, 86

Prometheus, son of Iapetos: 4, 11, 16, 29, 47, 61-68, 71, 97–100

Rhea, mother of Zeus: 32, 56–57

Ring-composition: 15–16, 47, 86

Semele, mother of Dionysos: 87–88

Shame: will abandon men of the iron race, 104; bad kind of, 112; how Shamelessness defeats, 113

Styx: birth of, 48; she and her children (Zelos, Nike, Kratos, and Bia) honored by Zeus, 49–53, 55, 85; gods swear by water of, 76–78

Success *(Arete):* 111–12

Succession Myth: 8–9, 33, 37–38, 53, 59, 71, 85, 105

Themis, mother of Horai and Moirai: 32, 39, 84–86

Thetis: daughter of Nereus, 41; mother of Achilleus, 89

Triads: 51–52, 59

Typhoeus (Typhaon, Typhon): Near Eastern origin of, 8–9, 47; mates with Echidna, 45–46; defeated by Zeus, 78–83; wild winds arise from, 52, 82

Zeus: 4, 8–10, 12–16, 23–30, 33–34, 37–39, 47–61, 63–90, 93–94, 96–103, 108–110, 113, 115, 118, 120–22, 126, 130–31, 133, 136; apportions honors to other divinities, 26, 48–49, 52–55, 83, 85; *aristeia* against Titans, 72–74; *aristeia* against Typhoeus, 80–82; god of justice, 93–94, 96, 108–110, 113; his mind unsearchable, 115, 121–22; Chthonian, 120, 122; sender of the days, 139